$10.95

Identification & Value Guide To

COUNTRY STORE ANTIQUES

by Lar Hothem

ISBN 0-89689-045-7

i

ACKNOWLEDGEMENTS

The writer gladly acknowledges the assistance given by many persons in researching and preparing this book. Names of those who provided photographs are found in the caption credit-lines, but special thanks are due Dan Poore for good photographs of fine objects. Appreciation also goes to Robert A. Hodge and Jerome Hughes for additional photography.

The most complex chapter (research/writing point-of-view) is IX, where each entry is due to the dedicated help of a company or product representative. Specific names are too numerous to mention, but the help of these persons, quite simply, made the chapter possible.

Several people sent many dozen clippings from old publications, background information which appears in rewritten form throughout the book. Finally, very deep thanks to my wife, Sue, who provided good help in all phases of this work.

INTRODUCTION

One of the fastest-growing and most popular collecting fields is that of the country store items, often referred to as "store stuff". The small-town general store is included here with the rural or crossroads general store, since the "line of goods" carried was frequently much the same.

As known to collectors the word "store" can encompass closely related items found in such businesses as old candy stores and soda fountains. Some things, like cash registers, were universal and interchangeable. But the thrust of this book, and for most store collectors, remains "country".

The stores, and goods relating to them, are typical of our 1800 - 1950 lifeways, the timespan covered by this book. In numbers, there are more collectibles after 1900 than before. Materials from the very early years are scarce, if not rare. For reasons of availability, cost and appeal, collectibles from the 1875 - 1930 period seem to be most in demand.

The author's feelings are that a book on country store collectibles should include a great many things besides price-listings, valuable though they are. Prices can vary in different parts of the country, and desirability and availability affect prices. As in all things collectible, condition is all-important.

Just as the store was a general, not a specialized establishment, it is felt that this book should reflect a similar diversity. Therefore, there's a bit of history, description, photos of early stores, products carried, some interesting facts and a sampling of old-name favorite products. In addition, the reader will find a review of why store items are so avidly collected today, and tips on how best to acquire "store stuff".

Like country stores themselves, this is meant to be a warm and friendly book, one that welcomes the reader to this fascinating field.

LH

Table of Contents

Chapter I

THE ATTRACTION OF COUNTRY STORE ITEMS

Ask twelve people why they collect store material, and you are likely to get a dozen different answers. The writer did just this, and the responses are distilled in this chapter. The information is presented in no particular format, very much as it was received.

Nostalgia, to use that familiar if over-worked word, is indeed part of it. To reach and touch the past, however, is not necessarily bad or backward. It is simply to say that there are some things worth preserving. Whether for enjoyment, or for personal satisfaction, or for recording the past, the objects are valued by the present generation, preserved for the future.

Country store days really were simpler, less stress-filled, reminding us of vacations, Sunday afternoon picnics and ice-cream socials. There was, we at least like to think, a feeling of relaxation, of having control over the whole of one's life. There was a solid perception that matters would either improve or take care of themselves. There were, in short, few surprises.

Nostalgia, yearning for things quaint and old-timey, is still a solid part of our personal foundations. Country store days, if not fully in tune with our time, are still honest places to visit via the old store items. A spin-off of this is a close and intimate look at who we were, how we shopped, what we bought, how much we paid.

Our grandparents and their grandparents dealt with these objects, putting us in contact with our own past, our individual American heritages. This aids our perception of the past, and our complex lives can perhaps be clarified by the uncomplicated goods of the old store. Like memories dating back to childhood, if they are a bit idealized they are also uncluttered and pure.

Store items are down-to-earth products, American made or sold, from the people and for the people. The items were and are familiar, in one sense of the word, part of the family. We can identify with the toothache remedy, the cake mix, the box of nails. We smile at the outlandish promises advertisers made — and still make. It is our own pleasant folklore dating from times when most of the country was rural, horses powered transportation and bridges were wooden and covered.

Things from the store can also make us feel a bit superior or at least more modern, and there's nothing wrong with that. We can collect sure proof that we have advanced as a material culture in the past one-and-a-half centuries. Butter is no longer dashed in containers of many kinds, and the egg-candler is no longer needed.

Coffee is now pre-measured, pre-ground, pre-roasted, pre-advertised. Horse medicine is no longer kept in a special place, and a penny whistle is rather drab compared to an electronic game.

In prices, there's a certain fascination with what a nickle once bought in a general store, from a very good cigar to a giant pickle that was almost a tart meal in itself. Several dollars took care of a week's shopping list in the 1800's, and that was for a family. While years of inflation easily explain the whole process, the perception remains that goods were truly cheaper "back then".

There's humor in store things, too, in the patent medicines that were touted to cure anyone of anything, every time. Many medicines that promised to make people feel better had a high percentage of alcohol. This all was for the most part a deception that did mislead, but not too harmfully.

Almost all store collectibles are of high quality, the key factor of all worthwhile collecting. If any purchase "didn't last" or fell apart quickly, word made the rounds and business suffered. Store fixtures were made to be used hard for a long time, like tobacco cutters. Packaging was sturdy and suitable for many uses, a good example being the take-home wooden cigar boxes. When emptied of their rolled-leaf contents, they served for generations. They held everything from sewing needs to arrowheads, and the boxes turn up today, most in good condition.

There is an element of differentness that is also a store feature. Buggy-whips were the jump-start and cruise-control of their day, and clothes were dyed at home. Some dye packets were multi-purpose and could even be used to make ink for the schoolchildren. As store cabinets attest, sewing and dyeing and food-making were still largely home industries. Then, you bought the ingredients, the "makings", not the final product.

Astute collectors recognize that in many cases they are acquiring bits and pieces of U.S. commercial history. There is great fascination today in all forms of early advertising. Some company names continued and prospered (see Ch. VIII) while others folded, having failed to produce or price convincingly. Often the unheard-brands are more valued than the well-known, which brings in a rarity factor.

Store items are appreciated, too, because the older pieces in whatever category offer no deception. Tin looks like tin even when japanned, or black-lacquered or painted. Wood is wood, not a surface rolled-paint grain over composition or moulded in plastic.

Paper and cardboard are either heavy or well-made or both, from tradecards to store placards. No matter how minor the item, there is a certain straight-forwardness, a purposeful design. While "artistic" may not be the best word to describe store collectibles, or all of them, most store goods look good because they were purposefully made to attract attention. Many goods were rather bold, dramatic, highly colored and striking.

Since advertisements, for example, were geared to people then, they still appeal to people today. Illustrations of sipping cold drinks on hot days, couples in love, a tasty pause for a snack — these things have no time barrier, are still appropriate. So, they often come home again, country store to private residence, suitable symbols of both modern home and basic human needs.

And, store items offer the usefulness of then for the efficiency of now. Spool cabinets are appropriate for any collection of small objects like coins, while large biscuit boxes and coffee bins can hold anything from fabrics to canned foods. Large or small, some store object can be fitted into almost any part of the home. Usefulness never ended.

There is also the conversational aspect, because the casual visitor sooner or later asks, "What's that?". Thereupon, the proud owner/collector explains, in whatever detail. Store things tend to attract both interest and approval.

Cost is certainly present, and a fine aspect is the extremely wide range. One can acquire small containers at under a dollar or go for the grand and imposing fixtures for several thousand dollars, depending on taste and financial capability. One can indeed collect many smaller items, or make a great, one-time purchase. The point is, the choice is always there.

Store items are also collected by those whose families once owned a general store, and there was a close association with store goods in times past. Since there were many thousand stores, there are a surprising number of people in this category. Many prized items — store ledgers, string holders, cash registers — have "come down" from ancestors. And they often inspired the collecting urge along the way.

As suggested earlier, there are many reasons for collecting store goods, all of them valid. Each, or a combination, is very true and real to the collector. A writer needs many sources of information, and often overlooked is the simple expedient of asking one's spouse. This was done here; how in the world did we come to have over a hundred store items, big and small, in the house?

"They fit in", Sue said, "With our century-old house. They are not overwhelming, probably a good investment. But more importantly, they are easy to live with. They attract, but don't distract. It's almost as if they're part of the family".

Chapter II

THE STORY OF THE STORE

General store interior, showing the large stove, massive counters, many showcases and shelving almost to the ceiling on left. One corner contains the post office, a frequent feature of country stores.

Photo courtesy Milan Historical Museum, Inc., Milan, Ohio

The country store — and its near-twin enterprise, the small-town general store — began in significant numbers in the East and moved Westward. A few earlier stores or offerings of general merchandise are recorded from coastal cities in the South, but the Eastern Seabord by and large had the major beginnings. Totally American in origin, including lower Canada, the country store was a fine example of free enterprise in action.

While we think of stores as typical of great-grandparents' days, which they were, the stores are much older than a hundred years. Even before 1700, the foot-peddler was making his rounds. He was a sturdy gent with a huge backpack who walked the lanes and roads of developing America with light but valuable items. He sold needles, thread and tea, and dealt with whatever cash there was, for he might not pass that way again.

These men were known as "drummers", a word used for traveling salesmen even into the 1900's, because they sometimes had a small boy with a drum who noisily announced his coming. This of course was known as "drumming up trade."

Another name for these salesmen was "huckster", one who hawked wares, and large brass hand-bells are known as "hucksters' bells" to this day. "Tinkers" were a related breed, those who specialized in the sale and repair of metal household utensils, especially tinware. The name, however, is thought to have come from the sound of the tinker at work, the "tinkle", hence "tinkler", and eventually shortened to "tinker".

The pack-peddlers of 1700 became the horseback and wagon-peddlers as soon as there were more people, more buyers and more profits. The road network had improved to where a heavier load and wider range of goods could be carried, and the wagonman became a kind of mobile country store. In a real sense, the whole story of the country store is also the tale of American transportation.

Many wagon-peddlers, having "learned the territory", knew the best location for a store. This was often at a crossroads, where one could handle business from four directions. And for years, what we know as the early country store was known locally as the "crossroads" store. And some of these, when villages grew up around them, became a "cross-street" or corner store.

In the 1700's people began to "keep store" or become a storekeeper in increasing numbers. The site chosen was all-important and the business not set up with "trade" in mind soon disappeared for lack of customers. Due to a rural setting, most items carried reflected the needs of the people and the times.

Importantly, economic conditions became more settled after the Revolutionary War, and the business environment was more promising. The 1790's saw the first surge of such independent business, and by 1850 country stores were a rural mainstay, an institution. The store depended on people and people depended on the store. A great economic relationship had been established.

While stores in the East were springing up everywhere, a few adventurous souls headed West, some as far as the Ohio frontier. In 1799, a canoe-load of ". . . A large and general assortment of dry goods and groceries" was taken to a log cabin. Wares and foods were displayed on its front and on tree-stumps surrounding the cabin.

It was remarked at the time that the owner was a modest man, for he did not use flags to attract attention to his goods.

That storekeeper was not the first in the Ohio region. About 1763, a man went West from Pittsburgh, to trade with the Indians. He set up his general merchandise in the shadow of Lancaster, Ohio's, famous Mount Pleasant, known to the Indians as Standing Stone. We do not know if the man was a good store-keeper, but we do know he spent the next thirty years a captive of the Indians. Apparently, he was more valued than his goods.

The typical Eastern store-keeper — and later, those in other sections of the country — forwarded products traded by customers in his area to major wholesale traders. The goods might be leather, honey, feathers or meats. In this sense, the keeper was a middleman, and terms with wholesale suppliers and international traders (of tea, molasses, cocoa, rum, coffee) depended on credit. The store-keeper worked out the best terms he could, both with buyers and suppliers.

Customers "settled" monthly or once a year, after the crops were in and some had been sold. This coincided with the store-keeper's terms with his suppliers, and when he was paid, they were paid. If funds were not forthcoming, he was truly "caught in the middle".

Factory-produced goods, the basis of the store, did not get to the Midwest and West until the transcontinental railroads were completed and running well. Full-scale agriculture could now develop, seeds or fertilizers in and foodstuffs out, all goods moving cheaply by rail to new and growing markets. The canals had worked well, but were difficult to maintain and were limited in reach. Stores located as close as they could to a branch rail-line.

It would be good to mention that the general store as collectors know it had counterparts, both in time and region. In the West, the 1800's, it was the "mercantile" if it was located in a town. If it was a Western country store, it was likely to be an Indian trading post. Much of America had "company" stores that carried general goods, these owned by mining or timbering interests. And Canada's Hudson's Bay Company, with its scattered all-purpose stores, is known even today.

The largest numbers and the proudest success of country stores was between the Civil War and WW-I. With prosperity and the rise of manufacturing following the Civil War, there was an increased demand for all factory goods. Many store-keepers entered such divergent lines as farming equipment, pre-mixed animal feeds and household furniture. Some sold firewood by the cord, and coal by the bag or ton. Whatever the need, the store was there to fill it.

There were regional differences in what general stores carried, though food was always stocked. An Eastern store might have the very latest factory-made clothes, while a Canadian keeper might be heavy in animal traps. A Southern store would carry field tools, while a Western keeper might have both decorative trinkets and mining gear. Wherever it was located, however, the store was not just another business. It was a community asset, dependable, and with long-term staying power.

Interior of Barbour's General Store, with customer examining cloth in the yard goods section. Note game of checkers on the barrelhead.

Photo courtesy Department of Tourism and Public Relations, Saint John, N.B., Canada

The early owner, to succeed, had to have the trust of those around him. He could sell alcohol, but the wise owner was never seen drinking it. The keeper had to be a person of high moral character and have some education. His duties ranged from writing letters for illiterate persons and reading aloud the replies. Some keepers even served as estate executors.

Stores were important centers at tax time, when records were brought in and payments made. On election day, votes were cast there, and candidates came to orate mightily and promise sincerely.

In early country-store days, people bought things they could not produce themselves, like ox-shoes or coffee. In later days, they bought things they were no longer willing to make, like butter and jams. Special manufacturers came into business, with brand-names in milk, bread, knives and cheese. More and more, stores came to offer not just the raw essentials, but finished goods.

For years, even until about 1950 (cut-off date for this book) people still frugally ordered brown sugar in weights of less than one pound, a habit learned in the Great Depression of the early Thirties. The Roaring Twenties after WW-I did not seem to have much effect on the country store, other than to bring new demands for innovative products.

WW-II, however, strained the economic system of many stores that had somehow survived the Depression. Metal items disappeared for the "war effort". And candy and cigarettes went to military personnel. Non-essential manufacturing of all kinds was cut back, and ration stamps were required for sugar, coffee, canned foods, tires and gasoline.

Joining the War push, some stores became collection centers for scrap metal, kitchen grease for munitions, even milkweed pods to replace kapok in life-jackets. This all reflected not only patriotic awareness, but close ties with everything that was going on in the area served by the store. Any keeper out of touch could be, and likely was, soon out of business.

The times when there was a general store every few miles in the country and small towns had from one to several did not last forever. All along, traveling salesmen had competed with the stores, and railroad side-lines allowed them to penetrate easily into most regions. Whether individual operators or factory representatives ("reps"), they went to the people. They were the first descendants of the original pack-peddlers, America's first door-to-door salesmen.

The most important decline of the country store began after WW-I, when low-priced autos and better roads gave fast and inexpensive access to towns and cities. Now customers who had been limited to rural shopping could visit the large number of town stores. People could afford to be "choosey". Advertising helped convince people that brand-names were somehow better than a basic, no-name product. Many former customers would not go back to what they considered "old fashioned" ways and goods.

Country stores also had vastly increased competition which came from many directions. Sales volume decreased due to "super" markets, chain stores (Winchester and Western Auto were two), discount outlets for shoes and clothing, and the great mail-order houses.

The beginning of the end for many country stores was the Great Depression of the early 1930's, a time of numbing terror for those who remember it. There were few jobs and very little money. Sales declined and those stores which extended credit for purchases often saw more outgo than income. People simply could not pay their bills, and many stores went under the financial waters. As those who went through those times recall, "We simply learned to do without".

There were internal problems as well, which hit country stores wherever they were located. No longer was the ability to buy low, sell high and keep long hours enough to survive. "Paperwork" — rules and regulations — took increasing amounts of time for the harried store-keeper. There were more taxes, insurance was needed, and employee benefits required more time and money.

And, qualified help became difficult to find and train. Young people saw greater opportunity in the cities and were no longer willing to learn a little about a lot, for America was becoming a nation of specialists, and workers saw their future there.

Stores, already packed nearly to the rafters, had little space for the new products customers were demanding. Some — "convenience" or pre-prepared and frozen foods — required expensive new refrigerated shelving or storage freezers. The old ice-box was no longer sufficient. Ill-prepared to handle the new products, many stores simply folded.

Technology came into the homes of customers, too. Electric refrigerators and large home freezers meant that people could buy in bulk from wholesalers and bypass the middleman at the store. Often people bought in quantity at special low prices which the store-keeper could not match.

Another reason the stores ran into problems was that people became aware of a world beyond, this in two areas, food and fashions. A wider selection of apparel was available in the pages of the "wish book", the mail-order catalogs; and with the larger firms, all shopping could be done via their large stocks. Eating habits changed as well, and the old store lard bucket became obsolete. People were more health and figure conscious, diet-oriented, and bought in directions country stores had never anticipated.

Some stores adapted and survived, and a few exist today having been in one family for generations. What is surprising is that so many stores in fact managed to thrive despite great changes and economic troubles. The peak in numbers of country stores probably occurred around 1900, and the view of the old store as a turn-of-the-century institution is fairly accurate.

The store, its rise and fall, reflects changes in transportation, manufacturing, agriculture, financing and social life. In essence, the story of the store is also the story of early America in all its rich divergence and bright promise.

Chapter III

STORE LORE

An intimate look at country stores can be had by just glancing at some little-known facts. These are details that help paint a broad picture, a panorama of times past.

While it is quite easy to become nostalgic about stores, this is a more basic approach. It is schedules, prices, archaic terms, human affairs, business details and much more. Here is "The Store", seen from many angles. While the picture is not complete, and never can be, it is yet valid.

A number of obscure store-related facts was gleaned from the *Lancaster* (Ohio) *Eagle Gazette's* 1950 Sesquicentennial issue, a record-breaking publication of 400 pages. Many early business accounts were located in these pages. Special thanks are due Ron Johnson, Managing Editor, for permission to reproduce some of the fascinating bits of history.

In 1906, sugar was 6¢ a pound, flour 3¢ and chestnuts in the fall, 20¢ a gallon. In the early 1900's, flour was typically packaged in 12-pound bags, since much frying and baking was done at home.

Country store hours could be from 6 or 7 in the morning until 9 or 10 at night. The busiest selling time was always Saturday afternoon, when half a week's receipts might be taken in. Stores were rarely open on Sunday or holidays, or would have very limited hours, perhaps open from 8 to 10 AM. For Saturday, with much preparation on Friday, employees were sometimes given Thursdays "off", it being a "slow" day anyway. So for old-time store workers, it was "T.G.I.T.".

A few ketchup or catsup makers, actually a Chinese word, in the early 1900's added dye to color and starch to thicken the product, thus making it appear richer. Ketchup has always been tomato-based, thinner than paste, less tangy than tomato sauce.

In 1825, explosive black-powder was offered in two grades, "rifle" and "rock". The first was for muzzle-loading firearms, the second for blasting out stumps or stones.

Patent medicine names, if no longer believable, can still be amusing. Three "bitters" brands: "Dr. Shoop's 5¢ Preventics"; "Hamlin's Wizard Liver Whips"; and, "Dr. Bull's Salvation Oil".

"Dry goods" in a store were clothing and fabrics; "wet goods", on the other hand, meant whisky or other intoxicating beverages, which many storekeepers refused to sell. It was not so much a moral or ethical decision, but a monetary one. In early days, customers expected a free swig in return for their business, so the owner rarely made money on the keg. Plus, rowdy drinkers tended to keep the "better trade" away.

Kerosene, the staple of home lighting in lamps with wicks, was once known as "coal-oil" or "carbon-oil". Kerosene gradually replaced whale oil, known simply as "sperm" after the whale of that name, because it was cheaper, more plentiful and nearly as good.

Store accounts were not always settled on time, or apparently, at all. One 1847 newspaper advertisement/notice requested that the customers ". . . pay us our dues. . .". The owners then threatened that if bills were not settled, they would be forced to ". . . go elsewhere to seek our bread and butter and meat".

Children in country store days teased one another with many fears. One was that they would be stolen by gypsies. Another was the giant spider which was rumored to lurk in the store's hanging "hand" of bananas.

In 1809, a Midwestern log store and adjacent home were purchased for a total of 60 dollars. Beginning, the entire store stock was held on one board shelf, 12 feet long, one foot wide. Receipts at first averaged two dollars a day.

Coffee beans once were not widely available, and very expensive or "pricey". And, it was often a "cash-only" item. To cope, people made teas from sassafras (a sapling's roots) and spearmint (a low herb, leaves and higher stems). Coffee substitutes were made by scorching rye, wheat or other field-grains in a skillet, then grinding the grain.

As a public-safety measure, general stores in small towns were sometimes restricted by ordinance as to the amount of black-powder that could be kept on hand. One 1831 law put the limit at 28 pounds of powder, to be kept in no fewer than two cannisters of (non-sparking) tin or copper. Fines for disobedience were not to exceed $25.

In 1850, a common price for live hogs was $1.25 to $1.90 per hundred pounds. The early 1830's saw uncleared land (forest) sell for $8 an acre, more if timbered or cleared. Corn was 5¢ to 12¢ a bushel, delivered. In the late 1820's, the best beef sold, already butchered, for 3¢ a pound.

In 1826, an European duke visited New Lancaster (now Lancaster, Ohio) and described a general store in the small town. "...Such a store in America contains a great variety of articles: All kinds of dry goods, porcelain, earthware, glasses, stationery, implements of husbandry, iron wares, saddlery, and spirits; the latter are only by wholesale; also, school-books, bibles, and psalm-books."

Many stores kept three grades of sweet syrup in stock, good, better and best. The lowest was Blackstrap, a dark and very thick grade, sometimes used as an ingredient in cattle feed. It was also for table use, strong but cheap. Sorghum from cane was widely used, and was the average-grade purchase. The best grade was known as "New Orleans", from fine Southern sugar cane. The best grade of all, kept in a few larger stores, was the imported "Extra-Fine Barbados", light, golden and expensive. An equivalent today would be refined honey.

A typical country store in the late 1800's could be run by four persons, the storekeeper or owner, and his assistants. While one-man operations were not unusual, these were more typical of early days. The apprentice was a young man of promise, possibly a relative, "learning the business". A chore-boy did pickup, delivery, cleaning and restocking. The clerk was generally the main salesperson, who sometimes "did the books" as well. But usually the owner had this crucial job, at least weekly totals, as well as stock reordering.

"Store-bought" or "store-boughten" was once a proud phrase, meaning the possessor of the item had modern taste and "cash money". There were two criteria for anything so-described: It had to be a manufactured product, and, purchased at retail price.

The store's "dry goods" section — also called "soft goods" — consisted of textiles, clothing and related items. This special counter or department was begun in the 1850-75 period, and offered calico, sheeting, drill (cotton or linen twill, used for sturdy work clothing), lace, ribbons, and so forth.

In the third quarter of the 1800's, "made up" or ready-made and factory-sized shoes were added to store stock. Shoes for the first time can in "boot boxes". Shoes and boots were by then shaped to the left and right feet; previously, one last had been used to build the shoes to fit either foot.

The first paper wrappers in a country store were heavy brown sheets about two feet square. Bulk purchases were dumped in the center, and the corners tied with string. After the Civil War, true bags or sacks were pre-made in some stores during slack times, after the rush of business.

One of the more unusual general stores in America operated from 1904 until 1936. It carried a line ranging from all-day-suckers to furniture, but specialized in staples and groceries. With a length of 24 feet and a width of only 6, it was a boat used on Ohio's Buckeye Lake, originally a canal reservoir. Waterfront homes were served, and four trips a week were made with as many as 150 stops a day. Un-country store problems included running aground, spills into the water, and a tornado-produced waterspout.

In 1847, hats and caps were available in many styles, and the price range was from 12½¢ to $4.

Loose or grain sugar in early times came in 300-lb. barrels or 100-lb. burlap sacks. It was either placed in a bulk bin or scooped into 1, 2 or 5-lb. packages. During canning season, sugar came to be sold in 25-lb. muslin bags, for making jams, jellies or as a food preservative. Salt also came in barrels of about 300 lbs., and was usually area-made at a salt-water spring.

In the early 1900's, stores generally carried four kinds of salt. One was "granulated table" for food and seasoning, while large, square solid blocks with a bottom stake-hole were "cattle licks". Small, round blocks were purchased by the many people who raised tame rabbits as a food source, and this salt was known as "bunny spools". Epsom salt, or hydrated magnesium sulphate, was used as a cathartic for both people and animals, and sold for 10¢ a pound.

Some stores sold burial markers in the 1840's, and they could be had in several varieties and prices. Head and foot stones were $2 to $10, "mural tables" $3 to $12. Flat tombstones were $5 to $80, while monuments were $6 to $100.

In 1900, there were probably more than 20,000 different brands of chewing and smoking tobacco, for "chaws", snuff, pipes, cigars and cigarettes. This explains the wealth of tobacco-related collectibles. Tin tobacco tags were once used either as brand-name markers or as prizes or premiums.

Name-brand coffee floor display units, wooden, were large bins with slanting tops, also used as shipping containers. Many examples were designed to hold 120 pounds of coffee, made up in one-lb. paper bags. These are popular with collectors because of the still-useful storage capacity.

Until just before 1850, the small-town general store could be located by name only, and new, would-be customers were confused by directions to it. And then, some wise soul decided that numbering businesses made sense, and would make it easier for all concerned. Before long, at least in the Midwest, street numbers came into being-and business directories began to be published.

About 1860, garden and flower seeds first became available in dainty packets with premeasured contents. Package fronts had colorful pictures of what the plants produced, or were supposed to. Many seed boxes served as both shipping containers and store display units.

Store cigars were typically of three grades. Good cigars were the harsh "stogies", first smoked by Conestoga wagon drivers, and

16

"tobys", sweetened with molasses. Better brands were made from straight or blended domestic tobaccos. The very best brands were imported hand-rolled Cuban cigars.

A mid-1800's advertising slogan: "Dinmore's Soap washes everything but morals and conscience".

In 1900, bicycles were very popular and "wheelmen" cycling clubs were everywhere. Three of the best "bike" makes were Featherstone, Rambler and Tribune.

Many country stores sold books, and in the 1840's, these titles were available: *Lynch's Expedition To The Dead Sea; Life of John Quincy Adams; McCauley's Essays and Views; The Woodman;* and *Pilgrims In The Shadow Of Sangtrau.* Novels included *The Sea Lions,* and *The Retribution.*

In 1849, a year in which many storekeepers closed shop and headed for the California gold fields, a saddle cost $14 and up, while a set of buggy harness started at $11.

Store owners of all periods were aware of mouse damage and the unsightly litter they caused. Mouse-traps of several kinds were kept in strategic places, perhaps near the cheese or crackers. Some traps were the spring-bar kill types, while others were quite decorative and captured the creatures alive for amusement. Some even had tiny exercise wheels. The best trap of all was a store cat that seemed to sleep most of the time. Such stores, however, had no mice.

Potatoes were a basic food source, and their popularity is reflected by the container sizes in which they were sold. Usually, these were the five: Half-peck (7½ lb.), peck, half-bushel, bushel (60 lb.) and 100-lb. burlap sack. Potatoes could also be purchased by the pound in most stores.

Store "freebies" were often given to children when the bill was "settled" or paid up. There were three common original store giveaways. They were, half a weiner, the small "lady's fingers" bananas from the top of the bunch, or a paper "poke" of candy. This last was a paper pocket for the candy, sometimes poked into cone-shape by the clerk.

Stoneware crocks were always available in country stores, and the best-selling sizes were from 2 to 10 gallons. The early 1900's price was 50¢ a gallon, or, $1 for the first example, $5 for the second.

Before Rural Free Delivery (RFD), post offices were often in one corner of the country store. Proprietors made little money by also serving as postmaster, but welcomed the facility because it brought trade to the store. Early boxes rented for as little as five cents for three months. The mail was sometimes sorted in an empty tobacco box. Children often picked up mail on the way home from school.

Before 1883, storekeepers kept time and set store hours based on the prevailing practice of their region, this judged only by the sun's position. For efficiency and precision, the railroads in November 18th of that year tried an unheard-of idea — time zones. The country was divided into four zones, Eastern, Central, Mountain and Pacific. Regions within the zones slowly accepted the concept, but some resisted. The system was only officially adopted by the government when the U.S. entered WW-I.

Most stores delivered orders, and a special regular-use carrier for a dozen eggs evolved. It was wood-framed and handled, and the cardboard tray-top was held by a sliding bar. In the customer's kitchen, the carrier was inverted, the bar withdrawn. The eggs were left in the sectioned tray, which then became a storage unit.

For years in the 1800's, people frugally ordered staples like brown sugar in quantities of less than one pound, due to tight money. This habit continued into, and was reinforced by, the Great Depression.

In the late 1800's, fans and parasols became popular store stock. Both were used out-of-doors to protect a woman's delicate features from the sun. A parasol was not an umbrella; the word is Spanish, "for the sun", and kept milady's face milk-white. A tan face then was the sign of a woman who worked in the fields and was considered lower-class. Bonnets were used for the same purpose.

A "loss leader" or "leader" was any store commodity offered at cost or less in order to attract customers. One early merchant specialized in "butter crackers", two pounds for 15¢. Merchants tried to sell crackers as fast as they got them so the stock was always fresh.

Mutton-tallow and neatsfoot oil were always popular sellers. They were used to soften and preserve boots and working shoes, and other heavy leather goods. Neatsfoot oil is light, rendered oil from the feet of cattle, and is still sold today.

Storekeepers, if their area had few customers, had other jobs as well, often two or more. Known "extra" positions were: Barber, "under-taker" (not a mortician, but one who undertook to do many kinds of work); freight-master, grave-digger, blacksmith, mortician, coal-hauler and grain elevator operator.

The biggest change in marketing store goods was in the 1860's to 1880's period. The shift was from bulk goods to packages, barrels to cartons, and wood to cardboard and paper. The container business quickly developed. The new materials and shapes were easier to store, required less effort to get when sold (pre-weighed or measured amounts), and customers liked the new packages. And, importantly, there was room on the packages for advertising the growing number of brand names.

Since the store often functioned as a post-office, the keeper had to know the special letter rates for distances. In the early 1800's, these ranged from 1¼ cents (under 50 miles) to 25 cents (for anywhere in the states that existed at that time). Postage was rarely paid in advance, but by the recipient of the letter. Only relatively important messages were sent.

Baking powder first became widely accepted in the 1850's. All brands were based on one of three ingredients: Alum, cream of tartar (from grapes), or phosphate.

Gasoline, before 1914, was sold from hand-operated pumps that forced the fuel up into a large glass holding tank. It also served as a liquid measure, and filled the customer's tank by gravity. Some examples survived in operation into the early 1940's. Gulf's first drive-up gas station was opened in 1914, in Pittsburgh.

An 1820 washing machine, invented by one A. Alexander, was extolled in these words: "On this machine you can full your linsey, flannel, blankets, etc. as much as six yards at a time, more or less." Regarding payment for its use, "One-half will be received in country product, and the other half cash".

The general store might be said to have had patriotic grapes. The favorite grape varieties were red (Delaware), white (Niagara), and blue (Concord). The last was more nearly a purple grape, and many people grew them in home grape arbors.

The "notion" part of a store sign — which also came to mean "idea" in common language — referred to small items of household use. These included buttons, thread, thimbles (from "thumb bells"), ribbons, and all sewing-related objects.

Some states had laws that prohibited the shop-keeper from touching (for the sake of sanitation) tobacco products before they were sold. Thus, a unique tobacco showcase developed, one with a level to the side and rear. The owner pushed down on this, which raised the case front or top, allowing the customer to reach in and "help himself" to whatever he wished. The showcase was an added expense, but both law and business needs were satisfied.

Sun-dried plums became prunes, which in turn came into the store in large wooden boxes. These had special stenciled markings on sides and front, like "30-40" or "70-80". This indicated prune size, giving how many it took to make a pound.

White sugar sometimes came in a solid mass in very early store days, packed in a wooden barrel. The sugar had to be broken out with large corkscrew-like "sugar devils" or "sugar augers". And smaller amounts were either loaf-shaped or conical and weighed about 6 pounds. These were cut with a scissors-like "sugar nipper". This "rock" sugar was used in the home to sweeten tea, for cooking, or to make a cloth-covered "sugar tit" to pacify the baby.

Bold businessmen in a precarious undertaking, country store proprietors knew far more than they usually said. Directly or indirectly, they were very much aware of what went on in or near any community. In one case, when the local preacher came to the store to sing the praises of a nearby farming family, the store-keeper was not impressed. "You", he said, "Go in the front door and see one thing. I go in by the back, and see another".

———————

Certain meats — like salt-, sugar- or smoke-cured hams — would develop a harmless but unsightly mold in warm, moist weather. The astute shopkeeper had this removed regularly with a cloth soaked in vinegar. The process works well even today.

———————

Sealing wax was a major store item in early days, and not the paraffin used to top off jars of preserves, this also available. Red or other colors, these were used to seal postal letters after the invention of the outside envelope, well before 1840. The wax came in wafer-like shapes. Sold in small packages, they were softened with moisture or heat, and the owner's personal seal (often the initials of the owner's name) was impressed. Many seals were carried on a watch-fob. Sealing wax also came in bars or rods.

———————

"Cash and carry" chain stores began to compete strongly with the general store in medium-sized towns in the early 1900's. While "Mom 'n' Pop" general stores had an identical price for cash or credit customers, the chains tended to have a slightly lower price for cash goods. This was because of the difficulty of credit-checks, and the personnel were not usually familiar with their customers.

———————

Genseng, a forked wild root with alleged rejuvenating powers, was once a store sales or trade item. Also called "ginsang" or just "sang", the root shaped like the human body was purchased in 1815 for 7 cents a pound. One advertiser added, ". . . The ginsang must be sound, clean washed, and the curls taken out". Most of the herb was shipped to the Orient, and professional diggers sought the roots "up holler".

———————

An early liquor beverage, besides "hard" cider (with cider being a word meaning "strong drink") was known as "stone fence cider". It was a light drink about as hard as one could get. The recipe was simple: Four gallons of whisky were poured into a medium-size barrel, which was then filled with water.

The best thing about the general store was the conversation around the potbelly stove. Views of all kinds were exchanged, and one heard everything. Politics, religion, taxes, financial and personal matters, health, neighbors — it was all there. Gossip and firm facts at their best, the general store was the community center, just as the school was the learning center, the church the religious center. Stores remained open until the loafers had all left.

Most country stores were five-dimensional, with goods displayed front, both sides, floor, and toward the back. Some had an extra dimension, with items hung from the ceiling, so one was quite literally in a cave-like room of available purchases. Ceiling-hung goods included, baskets, tinware, hats and advertisements. Nothing too heavy went up, as the items were often hung from nails with strings or wires or hooks.

Early families lived by the rule that once winter broke, everyone took a "spring tonic" for health, considered a distasteful necessity. The most common tonic was a mixture of sulfur or "brimstone" and molasses, thinned with water. There was a curious belief that the more dreadful the taste, the better it was for a person.

One of the reasons a store-keeper liked factory packaging, besides keeping the contents fresher and being easier to sell, was that they helped reduce his "stock shrinkage". When crackers, for instance, went from loose in the barrel to sealed containers, hungry hangers-on were at a disadvantage. Before, one merely availed oneself to a few loose "samples". But later, opening a sealed package became more like breaking-and-entering on a small scale.

An interesting sidelight on cash or credit sales, from a man who operated a general store for many years: "We liked credit, because it was fair to us. If a child came in with a quarter for cheese, and I happened to slice off a wedge worth 28 cents, with the cash I lost the 3 cents. On credit, listing the exact amount, we made a slight profit. On such "low-ticket" items, our profit was counted in pennies."

The oft-mentioned loafers or idle men who frequented the store are usually portrayed as shiftless or lazy people who did not work. In fact, in early days there was little work that could be done at

22

night, especially in winter. Many were bachelors who simply cherished the companionship of others. They stayed out of saloons, and had their social center in the store. The loafers were often some of the area's better people, just relaxing from a hard day, and were among the best-informed individuals around.

In small towns, in store days, there were very few restaurants, perhaps only a small hotel dining facility. It was common practice to get the noon meal at the general store. This consisted of a nickel's worth of cheese (always "yellow" or cheddar), or bologna, along with half a dozen large, old-fashioned crackers.

People still recall with great clarity the store-keepers' special talent for counting eggs. These were brought in by customers for trade or credit, and the keeper or assistant counted by the half-dozen. That is, eggs were picked up three per hand at the same time, this done with great speed and never a broken shell. A favorite practical joke was to wait until some unfortunate soul was several hundred into a count, and then ask his phone or license plate number.

Early country store merchants were very concerned about the road near which they were located. Surprisingly, many were against improvements like paving. They did not see such things as a better way for customers to come to them, but as an easier way to go elsewhere to shop. Free enterprise, yes; too-free, no.

Two products popular in the 1880's were "Carolina Tulu Tonic" for respiratory ailments, and "Anti-Dyspeptic Olive Butter" for stomach problems. "Bag Balm" was an early treatment for cow's udders. It proved to be highly beneficial for human hands, and is still being made and used today.

When dynamite became widely available in the early 1900's, many stores began to "carry" it. More powerful than blackpowder, dynamite had two interesting properties. One was that it could be safely set afire and burned. The other was that sensitivity increased with heat. One merchant proudly ignited a stick in his stove for a prospective buyer, then slammed the door on his fine demonstration. The shock was enough to detonate the chemicals. Score: Merchant, zero; dynamite, one stove and several windows.

23

A sign of the times, this large placard appeared on the wall of a general store for an assistant or apprentice. "WANTED: Boy to learn the business. Must be strong, honest & anxious. GOOD WAGES".

Abraham Lincoln, in 1831, ran a general store as clerk for Denton Offut in the town of New Salem, Illinois. A general line of staples was stocked, plus dishes, calico prints, gloves and socks. Lincoln had a young local assistant whose major job was to advise him which customers were "good pay". Lincoln once walked many miles to return a dry-goods order overpayment of 6¼ cents.

Chapter IV

BUSINESS AS USUAL —
The Store and The Times

The country store was able to exist because it had goods people needed or wanted. These might be things not locally made, like saws or binder twine. Or, items might be shipped in from a great distance, commodities not produced anywhere in North America, for example, coffee or spices. The store was able to bring the merchandise near enough to be tempting to both country people and townfolk alike. Often the store was the only source, take it or leave it.

Storekeepers had to sell at a profit to remain in business, and some markups were 30 to 40 percent. Given the low volume of "turnover" in early days, this was not only reasonable but necessary. But pay-by-check was unknown and charging, being "on the books" had not yet come into wide use.

Instead, though it seems Third World economics today, trade at first was just that, by trade or barter, an exchange of one kind of goods for another. The customer brought in items that had some market value for other people or to the keeper, and a like amount, a sum, was allowed for store merchandise.

Commodities brought to the store included hides and furs, even scrap lead that was once worth two cents a pound. This was used to make balls for muzzle-loading rifles. Other cash-worthy things known to have been traded were hops, maple sugar, salted hams, wool, dried local fruits and handmade splint baskets. The fruit was pulverized and dried in sheets to make "fruit leather". Even firewood was exchanged, for the store's winter heat.

Though difficult to understand today, there was once an almost incomprehensible shortage of hard currency, cash, in early store days. The concept of a national mint with standard coinage and paper money was not widely accepted as a necessity.

The shortage of "cash money" and the high value of it seems strange today when 25 cents barely buys a good candy bar. But, 25 cents was once the wages for a full day's work, not just 8 hours, but sunrise to sunset. Normally this payment doubled at harvesttime, due to bidding for the best workers and the need to get the crops in.

Early store owners had to know monetary conversion rates both in foreign country coinage and between the various U.S. states. Until the 1850's, non-U.S. silver and gold coins circulated quite freely and were widely accepted. The common quarter-of-a-dollar was long known as "two-bits" because it was equal to two parts of the Spanish dollar, the piece-of-eight.

Money was so precious that, for dealing, silver quarters were cold-chiseled into four pie-shaped sections, each worth 6¼ cents, or a quarter of a quarter-dollar. (One who cheated and cut a coin into five sections was of course known as a "chiseler".) Commercial paper from come-and-go state banks was treated with suspicion, and altered coins and counterfeits were a real problem. The U.S. mints in fact began reeding coin edges so people couldn't "shave" them with a sharp knife.

In trade, the storekeeper did not always come out ahead, nor did he want to. Often a housewife's butter and eggs (for her special, personal fund) were sold or traded by the storekeeper for the same value paid. This retained her goodwill, and kept her on as a customer, with store profit made with store merchandise. The keeper thus had to be not only businessman, but diplomat and good neighbor.

Sometimes the butter, milk or eggs could simply not be resold locally at any price, because farmers had sufficient supplies. In that case, they were shipped to a creamery or wholesaler. Eggs were sometimes brought to the store packed in oatmeal to prevent cracking.

Trading or barter was a widespread policy until well after the Civil War, when two changes occurred which had been building for some time. There was more cash, and people were willing to spend it. But, they were not willing to continue with the hard work associated with producing goods for trade. Typically, they produced enough for themselves, and paid for what they could not or would not make.

The shift from barter to credit, later cash, was inevitable. The transition was from almost no money, to some, to a great deal of money in circulation, and it covered nearly 150 years of country store history. Credit meant that money, if not available now, would be at a known future time. Business was done with this understanding. We know this sytem today, under such names as "deferred" or "time" payments, usually for such expensive items as furniture and cars. In store days, even the smallest items were charged, and credit checks were simply by known reputation, good or bad.

Between the Civil War and the Depression, store credit became a way of life. Almost every family had a small booklet in which purchases were marked. These carried accounts until "payday", when the bill was paid or "settled up". The accounts book often had bold print on the front, with words like "Please Send Book With Order", so entries could be made.

Another common printing on this booklet was "Ledger Page" done with a stamp, followed by a blank. This referred to the other half of the credit system, the large store ledger or "day book". Therein, a duplicate record of the transactions was carried, as well as payments made "on account", and settling the bill. Having store credit was known as "being on the books", and most customers were. If a person was unknown or untrustworthy, it was strictly, "cash and carry".

Day book entries contain the usual listing of goods bought, but some references show that the storekeeper was concerned about the lives of his customers. One 1921 ledger notation: "Shoes for Mrs. D., shoes for Virginia, 15, or she has to stay out of school."

A 1903-04 store ledger carries entries of credit sales, plus regular updates of who paid and how much. Payments of only a few cents are faithfully recorded, each identified with the words "To cash", or, "By cash". According to this record, it was not uncommon for a neighbor to send account money along with a friend who was "going to the store".

While trading, if the value of produce bought was less than the value of the goods brought in by the customer, a "credit due" bill was issued. This was to be used the next time the customer came to the store. Haggling or seeking a lower price was not unheard of, especially for expensive things like a new set of horse harness or several 100-pound bags of beet or cane sugar. Such tactics were likely to be successful if the owner had a nearby competitor, and the customer was able to get a price reduction.

In early days, because of currency shortages, stores had no need for a special cash container. A ledger, well-kept and up-to-date, was enough to keep up with business. The well-known cash register was actually the third method, following the primitive cash box and the later cash drawer. The box, of wood or tin, was a catchall for coins and paper money. The drawer was often in a desk or in a special piece of counter-top furniture.

The store changed with the economic times, either adapting or dying. If there was any "trade" at all, a store-owner sought ways to both keep old customers and increase the number of new ones. It was business as usual, and a business that benefitted all concerned.

Manner of payment is illustrated in the far right column of a 1908 store ledger, itself a huge, leather-covered book weighing nearly 20 pounds. Most entries are "By Cash", and a few "Merchandise returned", of course abbreviated "Mdse. ret.", as in "Credit for glass". "By check" appears frequently, also "By allowance". This designation may refer to "on account", or, allowance against other purchases.

"Raffle goods" was another entry ($5.00), which gave that amount of credit to the customer, the lottery prize winner. "Credit for overcharge" was listed now and then. Other entries include "By expense" and "By profit loss", apparently goods sold at, and below cost, respectively. Many customers made payments of whatever kind on or near the first of each month.

As mentioned elsewhere in the book, most store keepers gave small gifts when a charge account was settled. Those who bought all along with cash, however, usually did not receive anything. While the store owner saw it as a way of thanking for bill repayment, it did seem to be a way of rewarding those who took on debt, however small or necessary.

A rare glimpse of an actual general store in action comes from the store ledger, this for the second half of the year 1910 through 1912. This gives a look at the store as a functioning economic unit, a busy American enterprise. It is a brief study of behind-the-scenes, day-to-day operations. Note that this is not the "Merchandise Account", or bulk goods purchases, the cost of goods sold. This is the "Expense Account", and is so-headed in the original ledger.

The accounts are followed, exactly as they were written in pen or pencil, and they are selected both for interest and enlightenment. Entries are purposefully selected to cover aspects of the old store not widely known, and that explain something of its workings. There are several indications that the store was located in the state of Missouri.

The large day-books or ledgers often did not give the name of the store, or the town or state. These were private holdings, the soul of the enterprise, and the figures told it all to the owners. The facts, however, are all present — dates, names, purchases, amounts.

To condense the material, exact dates are not listed, only the year, item and cost. From this, one can understand some of the "upkeep" of the early 20th Century store. This is here presented in paragraph form. Some expenses, like rent ($42.50 per month) were regular entries, with others appeared only once.

1910

Gasoline (for lighting) 80¢; matches (probably store giveaways for tobacco purchases) 25¢; road sprinkling to lay dust, done in summer months, each, $1.00; glass cutter, 30¢; screen, 20¢; adv. in telephone directory, $3.25; annual donation to "Maintain the hitch racks", $1.00; freight on wrapping paper, 72¢; ice for Sept. - Nov. $3.65; county license, state, school and county taxes, $16.76; delivered merchandise for charity, 25¢; church donation $1.00; employee salary for two weeks' work, $13.00; Christmas gift for employee, $5.00.

1911

Electric and water bills, $2.05; store broom, 40¢; hinges, 15¢; insurance on stock, $1.00; hanging paper upstairs and in store, $9.65; 1000 letterheads, $3.00; adv. for "Chromide", $1.70; freight cost on barrel of returned paint-oil, $1.84; two remittance books, $1.20; galvanized bucket, 15¢; Eagle dues, $5.00; telephone messages, $2.30; freight on registered chicks, $1.12; returning "glazier's diamonds" (glass-cutters), 25¢; stamps, $1.00; newspaper ads., $2.25; "Merchant Trade Journal" subscription, $2.00; 4 road signs, $23.00; "Plumber, 15 minutes", $1.00; church donation, 30¢; lumber for repairs on upstairs floor, 45¢; electric-light globes, $1.00; donation to children's home, $1.00; door latch, 25¢; carpentry work, $2.00.

1912

Two phone messages, 30¢; 37½ bushels coal, $4.10; #11 cash register statement book, $1.00; postcards, 70¢; freight and dray (local, horse-drawn cart) on drugs, 96¢; show tickets, 50¢; sign on door, $1.00; painting, signs and front, $18.00; bottle, 41¢; Bowser oil tank, $92.00; "Craig's trip to Quincy", $10.00; desk set for telephone and messages, $6.55; freight on cases, $11.95; billheads, $5.00; newspaper ads., $5.00; bucket, 45¢; passing circulars, $2.50; collecting accounts, $3.00; one wall case, $30.00; repair cycle, $4.00; work on cash register, $4.75.

Chapter V

COUNTRY STORES — The Way They Were

Inside the General Store at Clinton Historical Museum Village. The store, located in the Museum Village ten-acre park, also houses a barber shop and post office. The Village depicts the life, work and social customs of rural western New Jersey in the 18th, 19th and early 20th centuries.

Photo courtesy Clinton Historical Museum Village, Clinton, New Jersey

No two country stores were ever exactly alike, so it is impossible to offer one description and say with confidence that this is *the* store. Businesses varied greatly from one era to another and in geographic areas of the country. Even the size made an important difference, as large stores had a greater range of products, while smaller stores stayed with the basics.

Even in the same locality, a country general store and a small-town general store offered some unlike goods to their customers. Not generally remarked upon today, there was even a certain amount of cooperation between general stores, trades to the benefit of both.

A rural store usually had a surplus of eggs, which were welcome in town. Thus, the country storekeeper might trade a large crate

Display of old tobacco goods, cigar boxes ("Cremo"), packages of smoking tobacco and large twists. People in eastern Tennessee once grew burley for market and bullface for home use, smoking and chewing.

of eggs for a small barrel of flour or some other basic commodity he was "short" of. So in a sense, some stores used other stores as a source of supply.

But with stores, there were far more similarities than differences, and wherever located, the general store had a certain sameness. Three aspects are considered here, and they might be termed "setup", "contents" and "operation".

The "general" store was so-called because it was a general-merchandise store, stocking and stacking a little of just about everything. In non-necessities, the merchant could not carry a wide range of grades, but kept one average type or brand. Because only one store might be available to people in a certain region, it was important to have a large number of items to meet customer's individual needs. This helped buyers and increased the store's profits.

Store setup was relatively simple. Most were quite long and narrow, though the width varied. The design was no accident, for this allowed shelving along the walls and this often from floor to or near the ceiling. Windows along the walls were almost unheard-of; though they provided daylight, they took away from storage or display space.

Medicine section, with dispensing and storage bottles, plus related items.
Photo courtesy Jerome Hughes, Chicago, Illinois

The basic store was sometimes supplemented by an unheated building in the back, or next door. Here were stored bulk produce or large goods, like horses' harness, fertilizers, roofing, animal feed, fencing, pumps, and wood-burning stoves. Also, highly inflammable liquids like linseed oil (for "doctoring", or as a preservative or paint base) and turpentine were stored there.

Additional storage space could be found above and below the main first-floor store. The building might have a cellar (under part) or a basement (under most), and if this was so, a door was mounted flush with the floor or slanted, in a special frame. It was used so much that raising it was generally aided with a rope, pulley and counterweight. Some stores had a second-floor storage area, and the goods could be carried up and down by stairs, or with the aid of a projecting outside beam with attached rope-wheel.

Most stores had either a plain front, clapboard, or the front had a central door with large glass windows and show-spaces to left and right. The door was fastened to a spring or coil-mounted small brass bell. Opening the door created a musical "ting-a-ling", announcing a potential customer to an alerted storekeeper.

The front display windows contained floor-height or raised flat surfaces, or shelving, and many goods could be squeezed into small spaces. Typical items were placed there to appeal to general needs — washboards, skillets, milk-glass nest-eggs, work gloves and buckets. Window goods rarely cost very much, and reminded customers of things they needed at home.

The store counter reigned supreme, and the word "counter" means a high, flat surface where money was counted and business transacted. The counter was a friendly and useful neutral area between buyer and seller, and it was narrow (for close interchange) and long (to serve many purposes). The counter stood between keeper and customers, and the worn tops show the polish and scratches and stains of years of ongoing "trade".

At least one long counter was along the side of the store, but sometimes set in the middle, enclosing an area, with counters on each side and across the front. A typical store counter might have cash drawer or register, cheese wheel and cutter, candy case, tobacco cutter, meat cutter, seed box, coffee grinder, and store ledger or day-book.

Beneath the counter, dried fruits and nuts were kept in "storeboxes", sliding wooden containers about 12 in. wide and 18 in. long. The contents went from the boxes to the scale. Dried beans and rice, for example, were always carried, because they were useful for many kinds of meals.

The under-counter storeboxes at a typical country store might contain the following commodities: Cocoa, coffee (bean form), sago (palm-tree starch, used as a food-thickener), rice, beans, ginger, pepper, indigo (blue dyestuff), soda, nutmeg, cloves, starch, salt, peas, sugar, cassia (tree-bark, similar to cinnamon), baking powder, malaga raisins (imported from Spain), tartar, mace, and allspice (also known as pimento). Storeboxes held commonly purchased goods, close for convenience.

The front and middle sections of the store had typical setups, but the back defies easy description. Probably not even the storekeeper knew exactly what it held, from unopened cartons to empty boxes.

Customers knew that two areas of the store were off-limits, the keeper's position near the cash and ledger inside the counter, and the back, the store's hidden closet. Simply put, there was usually nothing in the back of the store that was for sale, so customers literally had no business in the area.

One could meander to the rear, only to find that all the goods for sale were indeed "up front". The actual back of the store, the architectural feature, would have been known as "rectangular nothing". Unless, that is, one counted a simple door out for bringing in goods or in case of fire, or, steps down or up, in the "back way".

The contents of the country store varied a great deal with time and place. However, some goods were sure to be stocked because they were always in demand. These included cheese, crackers, flour, lamp oil (coal or whale), matches, salt, sugar, tobaccos and vinegar. The last was dispensed from a wooden barrel, with a tap for drawing-off into one-gal. jugs. Vinegar vats were sometimes used, with a capacity of 25 to 50 gallons. In early days, customers brought their own container for anything purchased, and an over-the-arm basket was a necessity.

For cold weather, most stores had one or two pot-belly stoves, the design a favorite because the round shape allowed maximum heat radiation. If a store had two stoves, one was likely in the dry-goods or hardware section, the other in the grocery section.

Chairs around the stove — except possibly a wooden armchair for the storekeeper — were almost a rare species. Instead, one made do with what the store normally stocked. Known seating examples include nail kegs, bakery bread boxes, shotgun shell-boxes, and 100-lb. metal cans of carbide.

As much as the stove or store counter, the cracker-barrel represents the old-time country store. In addition to hardtack or "sea biscuits", soda crackers (thin, square, white, made with baking soda), and oyster (small, rounded sodas) crackers were kept in barrels.

Other bulk goods were often barreled or "in cooperage". Examples include flour, coffee beans, molasses, vinegar, brown and white sugar, and coarse salt. Smaller kegs held liquor, paint or pickled herring, and these were typically ten-pound sizes and more. Interestingly, in the U.S. Customary System, a barrel, as liquid measurement, could only vary from 31 to 42 gallons.

And the store required two completely different kinds of barrels. A regular cooper made barrels for non-liquid contents, as for coffee, but a "wet" cooper was necessary for barrels that were to hold liquid. "Wet" barrels were usually of closely-fitted thick oak, difficult and expensive to make. Any barrel not needed in the store, if "wet", found ready takers among customers, who used them for everything from making cider to sauerkraut.

And just as a "dry goods" advertisement or sign was a way of telling people that no liquor was sold, further notification told the class of merchandise. "Software" was non-metallic. The "hardware" section — later to become a specialty store — had metal, manufactured goods, utensils and tools, locks and cutlery.

Cloth was originally sold by measure, the yardstick, and were known as "yard goods". These were sold also as "piece goods". An early phrase for quality in anything was, "All wool and a yard wide". The customer took the yard goods fabric to a tailor (suits for men, dresses for women) or a seamstress (who specialized in sewing). In very early days, the tailor was also known as a "seamster". Factory-made clothing, called "ready-made" (factory-sized) was an innovation and a costly luxury. Today, it is the other way around, and only the well-to-do can afford something "tailor-made".

Lamp oil was dispensed from metal containers in the back room, and these were never kept near the grocery section. Eggs, especially, could "take on" an oily taste, and were likely to be returned by irate customers. Often a small potato was stuck on the lamp oil spout tip as an airtight seal.

Large ice-boxes, set near the front door so carried ice did not drip across the floor, held eggs, butter and milk. Milk, known as "cow sap" to cheeky country boys, included top-milk cream or whipping cream, sour cream for butter, and regular milk for drinking. Whether home-produced or store-bought, early rural homes could offer the visitor four liquid refreshments: Water, cider, sweet milk or buttermilk.

Apples, onions and potatoes were kept in large, open baskets or bins on the floor, often placed along or near the main counter. These were sold either by weight or piece, and very large examples were prized for appearance, if not for taste.

Dried codfish slabs were leaned against the front of the store, or stacked like cordwood in large piles. This was a form of advertisement, and it kept the overwhelming odor outside. Several writers about early stores have remarked that these codfish slabs were much admired by neighborhood dogs, which paid their unique respects.

Other in-season meats hung outside as displays included hens, spareribs and hams. Pork was sometimes available in three grades, "cargo", "mess", and "prime", the latter being the best. Stores generally carried cured meats, bacon, hams and shoulders. Some keepers smoked meat to be sold with crackers for a standard lunch, and bologna sausage was very popular. Meat was occasionally smoked in a small building behind the store, called either the "smokehouse" or "hogsett".

Few store people ever knew the word "cuspidor"; it was always the spittoon or "spitbox" for tobacco chewers in the store. Set near the stove, this was a strong box half-filled with sand or wood ashes. Shipping boxes for five hundred 12-gauge shells were widely used. Otherwise, the pine containers were split for stove kindling or given away to customers.

A store carried "light" groceries along one wall, an area for non-staples like medicine, candy, chewing tobacco and store cheese. The early store had very few canned goods, except for corn, tomatoes, peaches and cove oysters. Some stores had bins for bulk goods, coffee beans and chicken feed. Early bins had lift-up, hinged tops, while later bins had roll-back tops or lids.

The store operation was usually a model of economy and common sense. It was kept relatively clean, with a damp cloth plus water and ammonia used for the show-windows in front, and the store display cases. Oiled and scented sawdust was used with a large push-broom to keep the floor clean. A turkey-wing or feather duster was used for store goods. For personal cleanliness, the storekeeper often wore a white apron, which reached below his knees.

In early days, customers arrived by horseback, carriage or sleigh, or on foot. Many stores had hitching posts or a rail in the front. Many small-town stores kept a wooden wheelbarrow for "fetching" goods from the railroad freight debot. Deliveries — and the amibitous store delivery-boy was once a local tradition — were made on foot, by bicycle, or by pushing a two-wheel cart.

Shop-lifting or customer theft was an age-old problem, and it was known as "pinching, or, the "five-finger discount". Storekeepers could guard against it from the beginning. If, for example baskets of apples or peaches were set outside, they were often covered with chicken-wire tops.

Inside the store, certain people might be escorted by a helpful clerk. In at least one case, the storekeeper bored a hole in his office door to literally keep an eye on things. Pilferage was one reason showcases became popular for small but valuable items like watches and penknives.

But, customers also had reasons for complaint. Some storekeepers were suspected of "double-weighting" or using a "heavy" scale for buying, and a "light" scale for selling. Or, an "off" set of weights might be used.

Conversely, some housewives mixed lard with their butter, or old with new. It took a sharp-eyed storekeeper to note the lower quality. People were careful about "sharp" practices, whether storekeeper or customer. Once trust was lost, it was difficult to regain.

Most country stores could be described as a dry-goods store that also stocked groceries. They were the first department stores, in a small way, with certain classes of goods kept in special places. These included cheese, seeds, clothing (work or good, "Sunday") perishable foods (grocery), "tinned" or canned goods, hardware, and so forth.

Baked goods were either supplied by a local firm or more distant manufacturer or wholesaler. Later, some storekeeper's wives made fancy baked goods, pies and cakes, specialties that usually sold well and could not easily be transported any distance.

Usually the first, sometimes only, hand-crank telephone in the area or village was in the general store. The merchant used it for ordering or tracing shipments, and the people for any important message.

Displays ranged from very simple in the early days to fancy later on. Nail kegs might have the top off or head knocked in for display and accessibility. A special clawed nail-rake was used to remove nails for weighing. Nails were sized according to penny-weight, abbreviated dwt. or pwt., equal to $\frac{1}{20}$th a Troy ounce. Tacks, on the other hand, were usually put up in small paper packs, either by the maker or in paper containers shaped by the clerk.

In the late 1800's store proprietors had large quantities of manufactured goods available to them, so they began to display more to sell more. Showcases and display cases were obtained, which were made with wood or German-silver frames. The fronts were curved or slanted so the glass did not "glare" and prevent customers from viewing the case contents. The showcases tended to departmentalize certain things, like shaving goods, tobacco, spectacles, watches and inexpensive jewelry.

The author noted in researching this book — having read a number of articles written by old folks who recalled the store of their childhood memories — that two things were mentioned with the most frequency. One was the dimness of most store interiors. It took awhile after coming in from a bright day for eyes to adjust to the semi-darkness.

Most often mentioned, however, was the smell of the old store interior. It was a mixture of pickles, cheddar cheese, spices, brown sugar, molasses, ground coffee, soap and tobacco. The smell was a unique and pleasing blend of sharp and soft odors, and every store's aromatic "signature" was somehow distinctive. Probably, most of the customers could have been taken blindfolded into any store where they "traded", and could have identified it immediately.

Such is the recollection of stores in time past — a business, certainly, but also a place of delicious sensation.

Chapter VI

FIXTURES AND FURNISHINGS —
Store Accoutrements

The whole range of items once used in country stores is now a major collecting field. These were objects that were not sold but were necessary to sell other things or maintain a smooth functioning of store activities.

Some items are easily recognized as "store stuff", like the large commercial heavy-duty coffee-grinders. Others, like shot dispensers for example, are both very scarce and not always understood to be store fixtures. Hard-to-find today are the cheese-wheel platforms or turntables, with cover and wedging knife, and very early display cabinets of all types.

Rarity factors (hence, value) of store furnishings include the quality of construction or manufacture, and, very much, the condition. Since store fixtures tended to be heavily-used over a long period, most were well-made in the first place. Normal wear (as, on tobacco-box lunch-carriers) is accepted, both on once-sold store items and the fixtures themselves. Broken or missing parts (on coffee mills, for instance) will lower the value considerably. No matter the item, large or small, condition is an important value consideration.

Cash Registers

When "hard money", cash, became widely available, it overwhelmed the old store cash-box. Something new was needed, and the cash register came into favor. Drawers held the cash, just as in the old wooden "money board", but with refinements. Numbered letters tabulated sales, displaying the figures to both the cashier (the one who controlled the money-box) and the customer. Later, a paper tape kept a permanent record of sales and totals.

Disadvantages were that some store personnel did not become proficient on the newfangled machines and slowed the pace of business. Advantages included a bell-sound upon opening to give alert that someone, unauthorized, might be "in the money". And, cash could be locked up for the night.

In early days, the cash register was a device to safeguard and simplify cash-flow. Later, they were probably purchased as much for their shining majesty as for more practical reasons, for they conveyed a successful image.

Values

Cash register, "National/Model 311", brass, restored.	$950
Cash register, "National/1054", brass, fine condition.	$195
Cash register, "National Mod. 130", newly cleaned.	$475
Cash register, "Mangold Brothers", brass.	$395
Cash register, brass, "National Mod. 130-B", fine condition.	$600
Cash register, wood, "Monitor", all original numbers.	$450
Cash register, "National", brass and oak, marble top, 1900.	$995
Cash register, "Michigan/Model 7", excellent condition.	$500
Cash register, "Monitor", wood and cast-iron.	$375
Cash register, "National Model 452", brass.	$925
Receipt box, brass, "National Cash Register Co.", unusual.	$240

Coffee-Related

Coffee has long been associated with the rural general store. At first the beans were "green", unroasted and unground. Usually, grinding and heating were done after purchase, in the home. And sometimes the roasted coffee had toasted grain added to make the grind "last" better.

Gradually stores began to receive requests for in-store grinding, and added a large-size grinder to the counter area as a convenience to the customer. This service was good public relations, and the fine aroma was a pleasant plus.

Some mills had a handle and flywheel on each side to be cranked by either clerk or customer. Gradually one handle gave way to a smooth wheel that accepted a belt connected to a power source.

Most store mills were of heavy cast-iron, large and brightly painted, with a patriotic eagle finial at the top of the coffee bean compartment. Grind was adjustable from coarse to fine, and a pound could be ground in less than a minute.

Values

Store coffee-bean roaster, "Royal", 25-pound size, rare.	$400
Coffee bin, "V.T. HILLS & CO./Delaware, O.", 32 in. high.	$155
Scale, coffee counter, cast-iron, 9 in. long.	$65
Store bin, wood, "JERSEY COFFEE/Dayton Spice Mill Co.", original stenciling on light red ground, 30 in. high.	$195

Fountain dispenser, "Drink Hires / It is pure", good condition.
$100

Lar Hothem photo

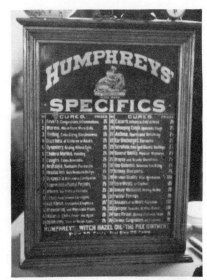

Store cabinet, wood frame, tin front, all for "Humphreys' Specifics", various cures.
$200

Private collection

Tea bin, "Emblem (chop) Extra selected Formosa Oolong / George Lewis & Co.", colors red, white and blue. Patent dated Sept 27, 1898, it is 13 in. square and 19½ in. high.
$125

Courtesty Robert A. Hodge, Candler, North Carolina.

Chalk board, "Natures Remedy/To-night/ Tomorrow Alright". Has gold border with red lettering, 17 x 23 inches, dated 1925.
$45

Courtesy Robert A. Hodge, Candler, North Carolina

41

Butter-buyer's sign, standup or hanging, cardboard, with changing numerals to reflect market values. It lists price per pound, and in store days could have ranged from 10 to 30 cents.

$19

Photo courtesy The Peddler Antiques, and, Thomas Collection

Store sign, tin, 25 x 36 inches, gesso framed. Ten-color lithograph for "De Laval Cream Separators", this commonly referred to as the "Milkmaid sign". Red background with milkmaids in corners, this is the rarest of many varieties produced by the Company. Excellent condition, marked "The DeLavel Cream Separator Co. 1910", lower left corner. Re-framed by Company for a general store in 1931.

$1000

Photo courtesy Dan Poore, Ft. Wayne, Indiana

Tobacco bin, small, "Sweet Cuba/The Kind That Suits". Tin, yellow ground, 8 x 11 x 8 in. high.

$85

Courtesy Robert A. Hodge, Candler, North Carolina.

Sign, "Glover's Mange Medicine", celluloid, blue, gold and red. Ca. 1920s, it is 6 x 9 inches.

$25

Courtesy Robert A Hodge, Candler North Carolina.

Snuff dispensers. Left, "Garrett Snuff", tin, red and white, 26½ in. high, 2 in. wide, 1920s.

$25

Right, "Dental Snuff", 22 in. high, 1½ in. wide, purple and yellow, 1920s.

$25

Courtesy Robert A. Hodge, Candler, North Carolina

Coffee grinder, counter-top, wood, "Challenge Fast Grinder". $90

Storage tin, litho. of woman's face, "Souchong Coffee", bottom pull drawer, 7 x 9 x 16 in. high. $65

Display case, glass front, lighted, "Maxwell House Coffee". $175

Coffee bin, "Dwinell-Wright Roasted Coffee", ornate stencils. $375

Coffee bin, "Millar Cup-Tested Coffee", 24 in. high. $155

Coffee bin, "Swan Coffee", tin, small size. $120

Coffee bin, "Clossett & Devers/Mountain Lava Blend", tin, 28 in. high. $145

Dispensers

While "soft" drinks — as opposed to "hard" drinks containing alcohol — eventually became the mainstay of the city soda fountain, some stores dispensed such drinks. Flavors came in concentrated form, and were mixed with carbonated water on the premises. Containers for the concentrate, the syrup dispensers or the mixed drink were in many forms.

And the store not only offered soft drinks, but other drinks as well. Hot or iced tea was a favorite, so also chocolate, hot or cold in the form of milkshakes, a beaten combination of chocolate, milk and ice-cream. Carbonated water and ice cream created the soda.

For the trivia-lover, a "malted"milkshake (later from the town "malt shop") was a regular shake with added rich and mellow smoothness. This was made from a soluble powder, consisting of milk, barley wheat flour, and flavoring.

Values

Dispenser, syrup, "Drink Moxie", mint condition.	$195
Dispenser, "Boscul Iced Tea", teapot form.	$70
Dispenser, syrup "Orange Crush", glass base.	$265
Dispenser, syrup, "Mission Lime", green glass top.	$95
Dispenser, syrup, "Hires Root Beer", china, hour-glass shape.	$350
Dispenser, malted milk, "Carnation", milk glass, tin cover.	$75
Dispenser, syrup, "Nesbits", pink frosted glass, dated 5-22-26.	$70

Display Cases

Many kinds of display cases were part of the country store interior, from large and long counter cases to small ones with one kind of item for sale. Large cases with several shelves usually had thick, flat glass sides and tops for viewing the contents. The large cases — sometimes remembered as "candy cases" — gradually replaced the long wooden store counter in some stores. Smaller cases often had curved or slanting fronts.

Earlier display or "showcases" had wooden frames while later examples had metal frames. Once the concept caught on, display cases became very popular with storekeepers. Goods of a similar kind could be grouped for ease of customer selection, and colorful and attractive displays could be set up easily.

Shoplifting was cut to a minumum. But the cases offered one great convenience to store-owner and customer alike. They protected the contents from dirt, cutting cleaning chores, and they assured the buyer of a clean product.

Values

Display case, shirt collars, "Slidewell", narrow, 4 ft. high.	$325
Display case, "Teaberry Gum", amber glass.	$40
Display case, "Remington Knives", 14 in. high.	$100
Display case, "Brantford Cutlery Co.", glass top, 18 in. wide.	$165
Display case, "Highland Confections", wood.	$225
Display rack, "Hohner Harmonicas", 1920's.	$75

Display case, solid oak, for ribbons.	$170
Display case, oak, "Balsam Of Myrrh", door lock.	$190
Display case, "Kaywoodie Pipes", wood.	$100
Seed bin, display case, drawers, glass fronts, very old.	$800
Show counter, 7 ft. long, original glass, wood ends, shelves.	$275
Display case, "Carborundum Sharpening Stones", metal.	$37
Knife case, with insets for two dozen knives.	$110
Display case, "Sheaffer" pens and pencils, 24 in. high.	$100
Display case, "Eversharp", wood, small.	$22
Display case, "Century Fountain Pens", oak framing.	$65
Display case, "Zeno Chewing Gum", wood, glass front.	$225
Show counter, mahogany, glass doors and top, 8 ft. long.	$425
Display case, "Auto Strop Razor", wood and glass, 6 x 7 x 10 inches.	$165
Display case, "Pepsin Phosphate", wood and curved glass, ca. 1900, 8 x 8 x 14 inches.	$225
Display case, "Barnum Cheese", glass sides and front, about 23 in. wide, wooden frame.	$375

Dye Cabinets

Special cabinets that held dyes, with the manufacturer's or product name displayed in a highly visible manner, were once in every store. They were necessary before the wide availability of factory-made and dyed clothing and cloth.

Dyes were needed because much of the "yard goods" cloth was not colored, to be made whatever shade the customer desired. Colors had to be "fast", that is, would hold the color when washed so they would not "bleed" or "run". Also, as color faded through use, clothing was regularly redyed for a new look.

Cabinet dyes were not only for clothing. One type was used for straw hats when they became bleached by sunlight. Darker dyes could be mixed with a little water (instructions on the package or on a trade-card) to make ink for school-children or for home use.

Values

Cabinet, "Diamond Dye", small size, tin.	$32
Display cabinet, "Putman Dye", tin front, wooden fram.	$125
Cabinet, "Diamond Dye", scene with children playing.	$575
Dye cabinet, "Dyola Dyes", wood and tin.	$175

Cabinet, "Dy-O-La Dyes", wood and tin, some packets
inside. $165

Cabinet, "Tintex Dye", lithograph of female figure. $75

Cabinet, "Rite Dye", tin, excellent condition. $125

Cabinet, "Diamond Dye", scene of woman washing
clothes. $450

Cabinet, "Dyola Dyes", wood and tin, good logo. $180

Cabinet, "Diamond Dye", wood, fine condition. $375

Store trade tokens, sometimes called "goodfers".
Example on left, ¾ in. diameter, brass, is good for one
5¢ package of "All Quality Mints". On right is a candy
token.

Each ... $2.25

Private collection

Store lamp, 36 in. high, milkglass shade 15
in. diameter. Iron harp with brass ceiling
canopy, embossed brass font. Retractable,
hung from ceiling, signed five times "Badley
& Hubbard", also, "October 30, 1870". This
was purchased from a general store in
Amana, Iowa, right from the ceiling.
Excellent condition.

$650

Photo courtesy Dan Poore, Ft. Wayne,
Indiana

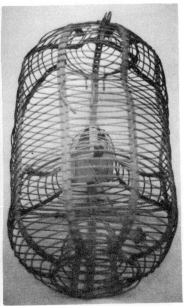

Store lamp, hanging, large copper reflector-shade, copper band, floral design in brass. It is embossed "THE JUNO LAMP", dated 1892.

$500

Photo courtesy Dan Poore, Ft. Wayne, Indiana

Wire mousetrap, a store item in two ways. These were sold from, and used in, early general stores. Length, 10 inches, near-mint condition.

$25

Hothem collection

Fire Extinguishers

Due to the often-isolated location of country stores and the large amount of inflammable goods — not to mention stoves, kerosene and a wooden-frame structure — fire extinguishers were very much a store fixture.

While this is true, there is a collecting problem in that many other places of business, even homes, also had extinguishers. These were identical to those kept in the store. About the only proof that a certain extinguisher came from a certain country store is an eyewitness account or written records of some kind.

The average fire extinguisher is not at present worth a great deal. The early glass "fire grenades" are quite valuable, however, and often had a colorful flame-suppressing liquid. Hung on the wall in special brackets, they were even somewhat decorative. Some extinguishers were a powder, held in a cardboard tube package, also to be thrown on a fire.

Values

Fire extinguisher, tin, "Richmond", cylindrical.	$23
Fire extinguisher, "Red Comet", with wall attachment.	$24
Fire extinguisher, glass grenade, "Clyde Mfg. Co.", early.	$90
Fire extinguisher, "1 - 2 - 3", brass, 6 in. high, bracket.	$26
Fire extinguisher, "Red Comet", metal clip.	$25
Fire extinguisher, brass, "Pioneer", pump handle.	$22

Gasoline

Once the general store was also the gasoline station, and many a driver bought store goods while a boy hand-pumped "gas" into the tank. Service at most stores consisted of gas and engine-oil sales, perhaps with free water and air supplies. True to its own history, the store supplied whatever a large number of customers wanted.

There are collectors today who specialize in gas-pumps and parts, like the decorative glass globes of the early pumps. Signs are also top items, with out-of-business brand names a field in itself.

For the record, petroleum refining is older than many people realize. Standard Oil Co. (Ohio) for example, or Sohio, had an oil refinery in Cleveland in 1870. Their first service station was built in 1912, with the customers driving in the front and out the back. A sign admonished "Drive In Slowly", and the station sold Red Crown gasoline and Polarine motor lubricants.

Values

Gas pump sign, "Indian/Gasoline", Zuni, 12 x 18 inches.	$55
Gas pump sign, "Texaco Sky Chief", porcelain, 8 x 12 inches.	$40
Gas pump globe, "Standard/Gold Crown".	$175
Gas pump lens, "Texaco Ethyl", matched pair.	$90
Gas pump lens, "Skelly Keotane/4 Stars".	$40
Gas pump globe, "Gulf", glass, one side blank.	$115
Gas sign, "Flying A Ethel", porcelain, 12 in. square.	$60
Gas pump sign, "Ethyl", 1930's, 8 in. diameter.	$35
Gas pump globe, "Champlin Presto", all glass.	$150
Gas pump nozzle, "McDonald/Dubuque", brass.	$45

Scales

Measurement of bulk store goods, from sugar to spice, was a constant store function in all business eras. One or more large scales were always near the counter and bulk goods, in a place where the buyer could watch the weighing process.

Today, one sees smaller spring scales marked with such words as "Not legal for use in trade". This was because a spring scale's effectiveness and accuracy depended on temperature, age and the spring's degree of metal fatigue. In short, they were inaccurate.

So, most store scales are of the balance type, counteracting the goods with various weight amounts. Interestingly, the 16-ounce pound is abbreviated "lb.", after the Latin word "libra". This was a main Roman unit of weight, corresponding to our pound, that weighed about 12 ounces.

Values

Balance scale, two brass pans, 1870's, fine condition.	$110
Scale, "Brown/1878", platform type.	$70
Scale, "Toledo Candy Scale", 1918.	$135
Scale, large, "Purine Feed Saver", all-metal.	$100
Scale, scoop-type pan, glassed round face, hanging.	$60

Shot Dispensers

One of the lesser-known store items, these were furnishings from the mid-1800's into the early 1900's. The dispensers were a basic wooden box, about 24 in. wide, 13 or 14 in. high, from 10 to 12 in. deep. Most had eight narrow compartments, each with different-sized lead pellets for the muzzle-loading shotguns of the day.

Each compartment in turn had a hole for refilling in the top or back. Each also had a bottom-front opening with a metal "gate" that opened to release the shot into a container, and a long front glass window. This visual aid let the customer know the shot-size, and the storekeeper could tell when one compartment needed refilling. Small, lower slide-out drawers held percussion caps in 100-count round tin boxes.

Typical shot sizes (smallest numbers meant largest diameters) were: No. one (for high-flying geese) to ten (for small, erratic-flying woodcock). No. five, by the way, was intended for Mallard ducks. BB was the same size as that used in BB-guns.

Values

Cabinet, shot dispensing, wood, eight compartments.	$300
Cabinet, metal openings, windows, wood.	$375
Cabinet, cast-iron furnishings, 12 x 24 x 13½ in. high.	$325

Special Displays

While the large and well-made store display cases were usually made by skilled craftsmen and were intended as permanent store furnishings, smaller displays were also everywhere. These often had the name of a specific brand and were sent by the product-maker as both a shipping unit and throw-away display. Some could be refilled and reused, such as the glass or metal types.

Displays of cardboard and light woods have not survived well, while metal, glass and heavy wood displays still exist in some numbers. No doubt — like seed and cigar boxes — some were used for storage purposes along the way. Displays have a large value range, from small and/or cheap to quite solid and of quality manufacture.

Values

Display bin, candy, lithographed, 8 x 10 x 11 inches.	$16
Display rack, for wooden knitting needles, holds 6 - 7 dozen.	$32.50
Display box, tin, "Boye Phonograph Needles".	$90
Display, "Dr. Scholl's Products", tin, medium size.	$110
Display stand, "Queen Anne/Fresh Nuts", folding, wireware.	$35
Display box, "Briggs Bros. Seeds", wood, label under lid, approx. 11 in. wide.	$50
Display box, "Rice's Seeds", flat, compartments, litho'd.	$55
Counter displays, "Sheaffer's", pencils and leads.	$85
Gum tray, glass top, "Adams' Pepsin", wood.	$32
Display stand, "Star Brand Shoes", small.	$23
Display rack "Morton Salt", for cardboard cannisters, 12 in. high.	$19
Display rack, glass lamp chimneys, wood, 48 in. high.	$85
Display box, "Barber Match Company", tin, large.	$90
Display rack, buggy whips, cast-iron, 14½ in. diameter.	$65
Display stand, pencils, "Eberhard-Faber", three levels.	$60
Seed display, for packets, opened halves, 26 in. high.	$50
Display box, "Ingersoll Watches", 13 in. high.	$45
Display stand, candy, brass, 8 in. dia., 7¼ in. high.	$55
Gum stand, "Teaberry", pale yellow-green glass.	$35
Display frame, "Opera Double-Edge Blades", 12 in. high.	$40
Display box, "Blue Jay Corn Plasters".	$25
Display cabinet, tin "Humphrey's Remedies", good lettering.	$70
Tie box, Indian motif picture, fine condition, cardboard.	$35
Hat display stand, metal, 14¾ in. high.	$19
Stand, "Teaberry Gum", clear glass, fine, unchipped.	$28
Display, "Chandler's Headache Buttons", 11 x 24 in., 16 individual boxes, 1930s.	$7
Display frame, "Master Padlocks", 2 ft. high.	$70

Dye cabinet, wood, grey cabinet with label in red and green: "Unequalled For Richness & Brillance Of Color". Piece is ca. 1900, 10 x 15½ x 17½ in. high.

$195

Courtesy Robert A. Hodge, Candler, North Carolina

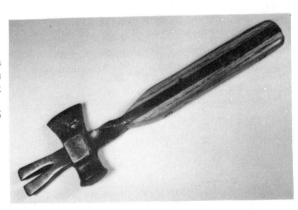

Crate opener/closer, a common tool found in most country stores; it had many uses.

$15

Lar Hothem photo

Display rack, "Wrigley's Gum", glass. $210

Broom display rack, wood with metal clips, 3 ft. long. $19

Store display, tin, "Adams Pepsin Gum", 5 x 6 x 7 in., 1911. $225

Stand, glass, "Sanford's Fountain Pen Inks", few chips. $15

Buggy-whip display holder, 1880's, unusual. $55

Display jar, "Mr. Peanut", six-sided, yellow, lid intact. $75

Display, "Resto Foot Cream", 11 x 14 in., six boxes, 1930's. $6

Rack, display, for hay pitchforks, wood and wire, long. $19

Store sign, 14 in. across, framed heavy cardboard lithograph. A ten-color lithograph for "Round Oak" products, of Doewagiac, Michigan. It depicts a colorful Indian (nicknamed "Doe-Wa-Jack" to help the public pronounce town name). Near mint condition, ca. 1910.

$300

Photo courtesy Dan Poore, Ft. Wayne, Indiana.

Spool Cabinets

Like dye cabinets, spool cabinets reflect their times. The non-existence of ready-to-wear manufactured clothing meant that most households made all or most of their wearing apparel, and home-sewing was a major industry.

Spool cabinets provided one of the necessities, a wide selection of threads. Other needs — thimbles and needles — could also be purchased in the store. Spool cabinets were usually fair-sized and most attractive in the store, just as they are in the collector's home today.

Spool cabinets are especially useful for storing small collectibles, from coins to arrowheads, serving a purpose their makers never foresaw but could only approve of. Since most are constructed with a cabinet-maker's attention to detail, spool cabinets are among the best-made store goods.

Values

Cabinet, walnut, two-drawer, "Brainard & Armstrong Co. Embroidery", incised in wood, 14 x 17 x 7½ in. high. $245
Cabinet, "Brainard & Armstrong", thread and spools, wood.$260
Cabinet, "Merricks", wood, slanted top, front drawers. $325
Cabinet, "John Clark's", three-drawer, wood. $285
Cabinet, thread, "Coates & Clark", glass and metal. $135
Sewing goods display case, "Boye Needle Co.", tin. $75

Large store scale with an interesting feature,
a stationary mirror for observing what's going on behind while weighing merchandise.
Store security is not a new thing.

$95

Lar Hothem photo

Large one-cent floor scale, "Did
You Weigh Yourself Today?"
Metal with porcelain finish, and
shield in red, white and blue.

$450

Courtesy Robert A. Hodge,
Candler, North Carolina

Advertising scale, "Use Bursley's High Grade Coffee, Best & Goes Farthest". Scale face dated
Jan. 4, 1989. Brass plate below spinner face printed "Ft. Wayne, Ind."

$140

Store scoop, brass bowl, copper fittings, secured to hard-wood handle; very solidly constructed.

$65

Unusual thermometer, "LENOX CHOCO-
LATES/ New England Confectionery Co.
Boston". It could register all kinds of
weather, from 155 degrees F. above Zero to
45 below. Condition is near mint.

$225

Photo courtesy Dan Poore, Ft. Wayne,
Indiana

Thermometer, "Ship Your Cotton To Phinizy & Phinizy,
Augusta, Ga.", dark blue and white porcelain. Dated 1917,
it is 27 in high.

$95

Courtesy Robert A. Hodge, Candler, North Carolina

Store registry or credit
card holder and file:
mfg. Shelby, Ohio,
dated (patent) 1914.
The `exterior is cast
metal.

$150

Courtesy Robert A.
Hodge, Candler,
North Carolina.

Store dispenser, "CHERRY SMASH / 5¢", polished sheet copper, soldered seams, brass spigot, lidded. Mr. Poore: "The value, in my opinion, is currently not determinable, since I know of no other like it." Therefore, value listing will be "scarce, if not rare".

Photo courtesy Dan Poore, Ft. Wayne, Indiana

Bolt cabinet, floor-standing hardwood, 144-drawer capacity.
$1000
Courtesy Robert A. Hodge, Candler, North Carolina

Shot dispenser, country store fixture, showing bottom drawers for shooting accoutrements. Note visibility holes in the eight shot-bins.

$325
Lar Hothem photo; courtesy Garth's Auctions, Delaware, Ohio

Tobacco Cutters

Long a necessity on the store counter or in the tobacco section, tobacco cutters are a favorite store item. Most have a cast-iron frame, and a descending steel blade that is lever-operated.

Some were made by companies that specialized in ironwork, while others were custom-made for a brand-name tobacco company. Such examples are "two-way" collectibles today, being both store furniture and an advertising item.

The cutters were used to slice off ropes or "twists" of tobacco, in the early store to a length ordered by the buyer. Later, chewing tobacco came in one-pound plugs, and was known as plug tobacco. The counter-top cutter typically cut off three sizes of "chew" — 5¢, 10¢ or 15¢.

Values

Cutter, counter model, cast-iron, "Boston Trade".	$250
Cutter, "Black Beauty", steel blade.	$45
Cutter, "Triumph Plug Tobacco", cast-iron.	$42.50
Cutter, "Star Tobacco/Griswold".	$40
Cutter, counter-top, "Star", 15 in. long.	$22.50
Cutter, "Champion Knife Improved", ca. 1875.	$135
Cutter, "Erie Griswold Mfg. Co.".	$47.50
Cutter, counter-top, cast-iron, "R.J.R.".	$75
Cutter, counter-top, effigy with dog-head shape.	$75

Packaging

Packaging was always a store priority for goods sold, and bundles were string-tied after being wrapped. There were many kinds of string-holders, some cast-iron and concealing the string cone or ball, while others were suspended out-of-the-way, from a ceiling mount with wire guides. String-holders kept the cord in a small place, ever-handy and tangle-free.

Usually, there were two kinds of counter paper for wrapping. One was a heavy-weight brown paper, used for bulk produce and for fresh-cut meats. (The latter were sometimes first wrapped in a layer of waxed paper.) The other paper was a smooth, medium-weight white sheeting, used for cheese and cold-cut meats. The papers came in long rolls, and were mounted on a shaft to permit easy turning and unrolling. Most units had an attached metal blade cutter.

Later store fixtures were the paper bag or sack holders, these also made in a great variety of sizes and styles. The holders contained from six to a dozen different-sized paper bags. The storekeeper

Store wall cabinet, very large, with 72 brass-labeled drawers. Solid oak.

$350

Private collection

Document box, sometimes used in general stores for business receipts. It measures 5½ in. high, 11½ in. wide and 8½ in. deep. If it had a lock on the front, it would be considered a cash box.

$19

Lar Hothem photo

had a sure eye for the bag that was not too big, not to small, but just right.

The paper bag was a development of simple wrapping paper. It saved a step by being pre-shaped and pre-sized, and was tight enough to prevent the contents from spilling.

Values

String-holder, cast-iron ball, pierced sides, ca. 1880.	$35
String-holder, "Use Jaxon Soap", kettle shape.	$115
String-holder, cast-iron in beehive shape, 5½ in. high.	$29
String-holder, cast-iron, cardboard string cone.	$32
String-holder and carrier, iron with eyes, hanging type.	$28
String-holder, "Dutch Girl", cast-iron.	$62.50
Roll-paper holder, wood and iron, "Climax".	$32.50
Bag holder, wood and wire, nine bag sizes.	$70
Bag holder and dispenser, wood and cast-iron, ten bag sizes.	$85

Miscellaneous Furnishings

Misc. is made up of a wide variety of parts or ingredients; after one tries to spell the word a few times, it is easy to see why it is usually abbreviated. Here, misc. refers to a great many objects once common in the old store. The section pulls together items that were in stores of all periods, with no attempt to categorize by era. Public phone signs and vending machines are of course later, fish-tongs and shot-bags would be much earlier.

Perhaps the main worth of this particular section, beyond the values listed, is the sheer information and wide range of it. This gives an idea of the imposing range of store furnishings that is available to the collector today. And, with few exceptions, these are "mainline" store items that can't be placed (like fire extinguishers) in "could-have-been" categories.

Values

Ledger-receipt stand with storage, metal flip-file top, underneath large drawer, "Champion Company", 48 in. high.$145

Pail, wood-staved, lidded, "Lusco Brand Mincemeat/Pittsburgh, PA", 20 lb. size, 14 in. high. $42.50

Coin-op., gumball machine, "Scoopy". $1000

Storage jar, "Planters Peanuts", football-shaped. $175

Dispensing machine, "Hershey Chocolate/1-Cent". $95

Tea bin, "Finest Family Tea", 9¾ in. high, bulk leaves. $80

Storebox, wood, "Monarch Prunes", large size. $17

Storage jar, "Adams Gum", lettering good. $90

Container, "Snowdrift Coconut", 10 lb. size. $22.50

Store-type seats, from 16 to 27 in. high. Turned seats, cross supports.

Each ... $15 - $25

Lar Hothem photo

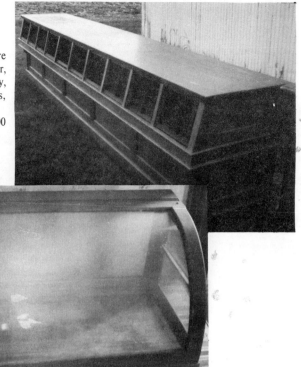

Combination store seed bin and counter, very large and heavy, ten compartments, quite well made.
$400
Private collection

Fine store showcase with curved glass front. Back opens down and is bottom-hinged with brass catches. Dimensions, 16 in. high, 35 in. wide, 18 in. deep. Wood frame is oak, lattice-work bottom with flat board surface. Name-plate is at front bottom and center, and is brass. "Graver, Kaufman & Co./Manufacturers of Umbrellas, Parasols & Walking Sticks".
$195

Hothem collection

Store desk, three drawers at top beneath slant top, five on left side, storage on right.
$325
Private collection

Store tin and display, "Feen-a-mint Laxative / Chew It Like Gum", 5 x 7 x 16 in. high. Brown with orange and blue lettering, it is 1920's.

$95

Courtesy Robert A. Hodge, Candler, North Carolina

Store counter-top dispensing cabinet, 15½ in. wide, 15½ high, 12½ in. deep. Heavy tin with wood base, brilliant lithography includes woodgrain backgrounds with litho photo of Doctor. Slant top, multiple drawers in rear for pills, etc. Banner reads: "I would rather preserve the health of the nation than be its ruler". Mint condition, never used, ca. 1895.

$1250

Photo courtesy Dan Poore, Ft. Wayne, Indiana

Food slicer, "Enterprise", cast iron, good paint.	$75
Penny candy scoop, "Germany", early, solid aluminum.	$11
Key box, drawer type, 200 assorted keys, brass trim.	$45
File cabinet, oak, 48-drawer, large size.	$450

Stamp vendor, "U.S. Vending Machine Co.", one- and
   two-cent stamps, glass sides, 10¾ in. high, ca. 1921. $400
Butter-box, bentwood, 14½ in. diameter, old blue paint. $42
Candy scoop, tin, early seaming, holds 8 ounces. $15
Clock, "Cat's Paw", electric, cat picture. $60
Scale-weight box, "Whiting Machine Works, Mass.", all
   weights from 100 to 4000 mg., nickle-plated brass. $35
Tongs, ornate, for taking pickled herring from keg, 12 in. long.
   $55
Food-slicer, counter-top, "Arcadia Mfg. Co.", adjustable. $85
Measuring stick, Ford gas tank, "Firestone Tires",
   12 inches. $13
Store measure, tin, funnel spout, "Maytag". $15
Ice cream scoop, "Hamilton/50A", brass, wooden
   handle. $23
Tub, tin, "Kahn's American Beauty Pure Lard", 5 gal.
   size. $30
Container, green paint, "Thomas J. Webb's Tea", 11 in.
   square. $45
Crock, "Heinz Pickles", two-quart size. $85
Ink, store-size, "Sanford's Ink", lidded, bail handle. $90
Box, "Quaker Family Medicine Chest", wood, 10 in. wide. $85
Dairy box, wood, "Consumers Dairy Co.", two shelves,
   6 x 11 x 13¾ in. high. $50
Spice bin, tin, "Benzal Mills Select Cinnamon", 10 in.
   high. $95
Blackboard, "Kayo Chocolate Drink". $85
Counter mat, "Stetson Hat", red and green design, 1910's,
   12 x 20 inches. $90
Box opener, "No. 2", cast iron, wood handle. $11.50
Barrel, "Cider Jelly", original paper labels, small size. $25
Vending machine, "Advance/1¢", brass front, 1920's, 15 in.
   high. $210
Store bell, brass on coiled spring holder, for door. $38
Storebox, "Louisiana Collars", rectangular. $9
Meat slicer, cast-iron, brass trim, 20 in. long. $160
Telephone, wall-type, walnut case, hand-cranked, 23 in.
   high. $145
Store jar, "National Biscuit Company", glass front, brass. $50
Crate opener, combination tool, "General Cigar Co.". $14

Tobacco bin, "Sure Shot", mint condition, rare.	$350
Fly trap, wire screen, 9½ in. high, round wood base.	$40
Bolt cabinet, 12 rows with 12 drawers each.	$750
Bread case, large, glass-fronted, hardwood.	$275
Clock, regulator, "Calumet Baking Powder".	$695
Bill holder, cast-iron, "National Cash Register Co.".	$35
Door push-plate, "Dandy Bread", metal, 3 x 13 in., 1940's.	$28
Store lamp, brass font, tin shade, chain cord.	$135
Straw-holder, sterling top, ruby glass.	$75
Container, front pull-lid, japanned tin, "Cloves", 8 x 9 x 11 in. high.	$55
Counter, 12-ft. long, multi-drawer, refinished oak.	$2000
Sign, "Public Telephone", round, porcelain, white ground.	$55
Shot bag, cotton, "Leroy Company", printed front.	$11
Storebox, "Jack Spratt Prunes", 14 in. long, wood.	$18
Stand, for credit book, hardwood, unusual.	$60
Clock, oak case, advertising, 36 in. high.	$360
Calendar, 1920, "Hercules Explosives".	$70

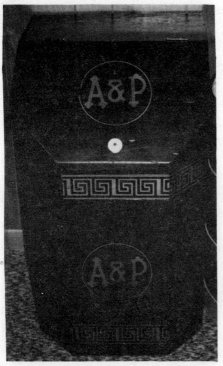

Store floor coffee bin, 32 in. high, 18 wide, 18 deep. Slant top with porcelain pull; construction is 1 in. oak. Paint is dark red with black and gold decals, maker unknown, excellent condition, ca. 1905. Made for A & P Company.
$375
Photo courtesy Dan Poore, Ft. Wayne, Indiana

Store stand and trays, "Beech-Nut / Candies / Mints / Fruit Drops".

$40

Private collection

Peanut machine, "Tom's Delicious Sandwiches/ Toasted Peanuts", about 6 feet high.

$250

Lar Hothem photo

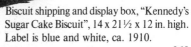

Biscuit shipping and display box, "Kennedy's Sugar Cake Biscuit", 14 x 21½ x 12 in. high. Label is blue and white, ca. 1910.

$65

Courtesy Robert A Hodge, Candler, North Carolina

Bin scoop, 12 in. long, tin. $30

Merchandise holder, "Watta Pop Sucker", dog form. $90

Store lamp, hanging "Aladdin", metal shade. $115

Price tag holder, "Nervous/Drink Postum", tin. $13

Store bell, brass, on coiled-steel spring. $29

Blackboard, "Whistle Orange", soft drink, late 1940's. $75

Wall clock, "Calumet Baking Powder". $325

Flour barrel, pine, 26 in. high, ca. 1870. $85

Seed box, two-drawer front, slanted desk top, "Vich's
Seeds", 18 x 18 x 12 in. high. $50

Store counter, ca. 1875, 60 in. long, walnut. $500

Produce scoop, tin, wooden handle, 11 in. long. $12

Clock, "Gulf Gas", 15 in. across face. $225

Extension "hand" on long pole, lever-operated, to take
stock from top shelves, maker's paper label. $30

Vending machine, cast-iron, "Matches/1¢". $95

Glass measure, for penny candy. $6.50

Candy jar, counter-top, metal lid, glass, one-gal. $14

Hat brush, store size, maple handle, 13 in. long. $15

Peanut roaster, "Empire/#1", 3½ ft. high, hand-
operated. $325

Scoop, dry goods, horn, very early, 9 in. long. $20

Box, "Cremo Cigars", 28½ in. wide, tin; shipping case
also. $395

Duster, feather head, long wooden handle, hanging loop. $17

In-store advertisement, cardboard, "Dead Shot Worm
Pellets". $22

Kerosene measure, tin, handled, 10 in. high. $15

Chapter VII

STORE STUFF —
Collectible Categories

This, by far the largest chapter in the book, gives some idea of the many classes of store collectibles. There are certainly many more than those mentioned here, but the chapter is fairly representative of items most likely to be encountered. For instance, for every long-handled store tongs or "hands", there are many small tins and containers, both home and store.

It might be noted that the categories were made up from individual listings obtained from antiques and collectibles shows and auctions, for the most part. Flea-market origins do not have the actual price-tag, as values tended to be either too high or too low, so a fair market value was usually substituted.

The specialty store collector will recognize that some collecting fields (like "good-for" trade tokens) and the multitude of individual brand-name products are not covered in depth. One day, with little doubt, books will exist on each aspect of the old country store, as well they should. At least, this book should give a broad look at what is available, and this chapter can give an idea of cost.

Advertisements

Ads., in the store, took the form of cardboard or heavy paper notices that touted a product. They were designed to catch the customer's eye and spark the urge to buy. Lithography and advanced printing methods produced artistic, colorful ads. that remain most appealing today. Early, plain (often black and white) ads. are quite scarce, being put out with woodblock type, and not many have survived.

Ad., "White House Melons", cardboard, 10 x 10 in., 1930's.	$7
Ad., cardboard, "Hambone 5¢ Cigar", 7 in. diameter, 1920's.	$30
Ad., standup, "Yankee Girl Tobacco", 9 x 12 in., cardboard, 1920's.	$6
Ad., cardboard, "Pure Gold Lemon", 4 x 10 in., string-hung, 1930.	$3
Ad., "Flyer 5¢ Cigar", Lindberg commerative, poster, 9 x 10 in., 1920's.	$36

Ad., cardboard, "Cupid Soda", Dolly Dingle girl, 9 x 11 in., 1920's. $18

Counter sign, "Pioneer Belts", cardboard. $55

Ad., "Country Club Cider", 6 x 9 in., cardboard, 1920's. $4

Ad., "Dandy Shandy Soda", cardboard, 11 x 14 in., 1910's. $26

Ad., "Dr. Lynas Hair Grower", 10 x 14 in., cardboard, 1915. $22

Ad., "Cyclone Twister 5¢ Cigar", cardboard, 10 x 13 in., 1929. $28

Ad., paper, large-size, "American Lead Pencil", 1890's. $100

Ad., "Rochelle Lime-Dry/15¢", cardboard, 10 x 15 in., 1920's. $6

Ad., "Heinz Canned Beans", cardboard poster, 10 x 20 in., 1930's. $16

Ad., cardboard, "International Fertilizers", 14 x 20 in., 1930's. $24

Ad., string-hung, "Fifty Little Orphans Cigars", cardboard, 4 x 7 in., 1890's. $8

Ad., "Perry's Soda Pop", 10 x 13 in., cardboard, 1940's. $7

Ad., cardboard, "Dr. Lynas Extracts", 10 x 13 in., ca. 1910. $12

Ad., "Portola Tuna", cardboard, 8½ x 14 in., 1929. $10

Ad., hanging, "Honey Razor Blades", 5 in. diameter, cardboard, 1930's. $4

Ad., "Call Again 5¢ Cigar", 8 x 16 in., cardboard poster, 1920's. $6

Ad., hanging, "Red Rooster Bananas", 2½ in. diameter, cardboard. $2

Ad., cardboard, "Cydrax Non-Alcoholic Soda", 5 x 9 in., 1920's. $4

Ad., "Green River Soda", 7 x 10 in., cardboard, 1940's. $12

Bottles

Quite a few collectible bottles come from the store, ranging from milks to inks. The largest field (see Medicinal) would be the patent medicines and bitters. Many foods, from honey to pickles, began being bottled in the late 1800's. Bottled foods became popular because some containers were capable of being refilled, lowering costs. And buyers could see the quality of the goods, while glass did not react with the contents to give an "off" taste, as did early tin containers.

Tin container, "Fleischmann's Yeast / Eat It For Health", box 3 x 3½ x 4½ inches, damaged condition.

$2

Private collection

Putnam Dye cabinet, put out by the Monroe Chemical Company, Quincy, Illinois, Medium size, excellent condition.

$95

Private collection

Tea container, japanned tin, "G.E. Bursley & Comp./ Indian Green Ceylon Tea", fine condition.

$265

Photo courtesy Dan Poore, Ft. Wayne, Indiana

Store tin, "Morse's Standard Tea", fine condition.

$85

Lar Hothem photo

"King Edward" cigar box, very common brand, contained 50 cigars, paper over board.

$6

Private collection

WW-II store matchbox and contents for U.S. War Stamps & Bonds. These sold three for a penny.

$4

Private collection

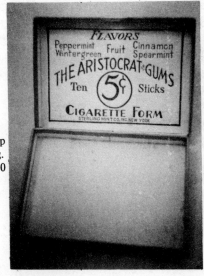

Interior of cardboard package for Gold Tip Gum, ten sticks for five cents; 3 in. long.
$2.50

Lat Hothem photo

Cigar humidor and shipping crate, "Buck Cigars/King of the Range/Good To Keep Good Cigars Good", lid lock. Brown with red lettering, 19½ x 27½ x 18½ in. high, ca. 1920s, scarce piece.
$450

Courtesy Robert A. Hodge, Candler, North Carolina

Bottle, cork-top, "Dr. Kilmer's Swamproot".	$4.50
Bottle, "Pond's Extract", cork-top, clean label.	$7.50
Bottle, cream, "Borden's", with cow label.	$7
Box and bottle, "Happy Home Glycerine".	$13
Bottle, "Atwood Jaundice Bitters", cork-top.	$11
Bottle, "Frank Tea & Spice Co./Castor Oil", cork-top.	$12
Bottle, "Snider's Catsup", ca. 1925.	$4.25
Bottle, bitters, "Electric", cork-top.	$4.50
Bottle, "Lydia Pinkham's Pills", original box.	$7
Bottle, "Wintergreen/Shaker Village, N.H.", full label.	$50
Bottle, intact label, "Tomato Ketchup/Put Up By The Shakers/East Canterbury, NH", cork-top.	$42
Bottle, corked, "Opal Vanilla", clean.	$2.50
Bottle, "Shaker Witch Hazel", paper label, ca. 1860.	$65
Bottle, "Burnett's Standard Jamaica Ginger/75% Alcohol".	$12
Bottle, "Humphrey's Homopathic".	$3.50
Bottle, "Sutherland Sisters Hair Tonic".	$35
Bottle, bitters, "Formerly Made By Moses Atwood", aqua.	$35
Bottle, "Colorite/Straw Hat Dye", some contents.	$5
Bottle, cream, ½ pint, square, round-top, no dairy.	$2
Bottle, "3-in-1 Oil Co.", aqua glass, early 1900's.	$7

Bread

Bread was long made in the home on "baking day", from store or mill ingredients. While the homemade variety was usually better, commercial bakeries offered advantages. The cost was comparable, plus much time was saved. In addition, machine-slicing was developed, and pre-cut "slices" became immensely popular. Before this, bread had to be carefully cut with specialized serrated-edge bread knives. Bakery boxes often served as both shipping containers and store displays.

Paperweight, cast-iron, "Pan Dandy Bread".	$23
Bread rack, "Holsum Breads", 30 in. high, two shelves.	$45
Tip tray, "Bricker's Bread", Mrs. B.'s face in center, 4 in. diameter.	$35
Belt-buckle, "Colonial...Bread", metal.	$17
Sign, large, "Hoppy Bond Bread", high colors.	$95
I.D. wheel, "Wonder Bread - - Guide To U.S. Warships", '40's.	$11

Wooden cheesebox, bentwood rim on lid, 16¼ in. diameter and 6¼ in. high. This held a single wheel; some boxes were about 14 in. high, and held two wheels.

$23

Private collection

Cap-boxes, brand-name containers and storage units for percussion caps sold in country stores. Original contents, brass cases.

Each ... $3 - $5

Lar Hothem photo

Tin containers. Left, "Geo. W. Helme Co. / Snuff, 1872, partial label.

$3

Right, "Geo. H. Helme Snuff Company", 2½ in. high, no label.

$1.50

Lower center, 1¾ in. diameter, "Bickmore Gall Salve / Be Sure and Work the Horse", full label.

$3

Lar Hothem collection

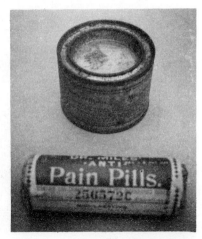

Containers. Back, "Horlick's Malted Milk Lunch Tablets", 2⅟₁₆ in. diameter, full label.
$4
Front, "Dr. Miles' Anti-Pain Pills / Contain no Opium, Morphine, Heroin, Cocaine or any other enslaving Drugs".
$2

Private collection

A fine array of product advertising signs of the kind that often hung in country and general stores. The Mail Pouch thermometer, of course was attached outside where passersby could notice both the temperature and ad. message.

Photo courtesy Dan Poore, Ft. Wayne, Indiana

Tin containers. Left, "Dwinell - Wright / Boston Roasted Coffees", 7¼ in. high, no label.
$5
Right, "Rumford", 5¼ in. high, no label.
$1.75
Private collection

71

Sign, "Hoppy Bond Bread", tin, bright, 12 in. high.	$70
Airplane, cut paper, "Butternut Bread".	$2.50
Friction car, tin, "Bond Bread", Marx-made.	$22
Plane, "Sail-Me Glider/Butternut Bread", giveaway, 1910's.	$3
Sign, "Rainbow Bread", embossed tin, 3 x 20 in., vivid, 1940's.	$20

Butter

Butter was another product that eventually became easier to purchase than to make. It has survived the severe competition from margarine, also called oleomargarine or "oleo", a vegetable substance with additives. Butter traditionally is made in 4-oz. "sticks", sold in four sections as a pound. The early 1900's were the transitional period from home to factory production, and most churns were put away by the 1940's.

Butter box, waxed cardboard, "Moo Girl", 1-lb. size.	$3
Dish, glass, "Bull's Eye Butter".	$55
Box, "Bossie's Best Butter", 3 x 3 x 5 in., 1930's.	$3
Sign, "Breden Butter", tin, 4½ x 8 in., off-brand, 1920's.	$22
Watch fob, "Meadow Gold Butter", celluloid.	$45
Box, waxed, "Bossie's Best Brand Butter", 1-lb. size.	$2.50

Tin containers. Left, "Magic Iron Cement/ Used for stopping leaks...", 1⅞ in. high.

$1.25

Right, 3⅛ in. high, "Calocide/ Special Plasters For Hard Corns", full label.

$3

Courtesy Fairfield Antiques, Lancaster, Ohio

72

Store sign, 15 in. across, framed heavy cardboard lithograph. It was a trademark for flour from the "Sleepy Eye Milling Co." of Sleepy Eye, Minnesota. This particular sign is very scarce. Excellent condition, ca. 1905.

$ (rare)

Photo courtesy Dan Poore, Ft. Wayne, Indiana

Candy

Before the Civil War — except for items like horehound and rock-crystal candy formed on a string — the country store had very little candy. A range of candy was difficult because it was both hand-made and expensive. The mass-production (machine-made) of candy began in in the late 1800-s and peaked by the early 1900's. This was the great day of the penny candy, and hundreds of kinds existed. Boxed selections for special occasions also became available at this time, plus brand names.

Tin, "Bunte Candy", 5-lb. size, store box.	$14
Box, cardboard, "Black Crow Candy".	$4
Jar, store, "Reed's Patties", round metal lid.	$90
Tin, store, "Campfire Marshmallows", round, lidded.	$11
Pail, candy, tin, Santa, dated 1899, 5 in. high, lidded.	$45
Cardboard house, "Charms Candy Co.", 9 in. high, 1937.	$24
Sign, "Chicken Dinner 5¢ Candy", 12 x 24 in., tin, colorful, 1930's.	$75
Sign, "Perrys Cherry Cluster", tin, 14 x 20 in., 1940's.	$28
Advertisement, "Melson-Berdon Candy Co.", paper.	$50
Container, "Angelus Marshmallows", tin.	$9
Button, advertising, "Bit-O-Honey".	$11
Container, large, store, "Bunny-Bons Toffee".	$60
Candy container, glass, original paint, bulldog figure.	$35

Chocolate

Chocolate is made from roasted and ground cacao seeds, with added sweeteners. It has been in use since Aztec times, when cacao beans were used as money. Americans have long favored a variety called milk chocolate, flavored with milk and other ingredients. Many kinds of chocolate candies were in the old store, and names like Baker and Nestle and Hershey have been around for years. An interest in expensive chocolates developed in this country in the early 1980's, with some fine brands selling for as much as $30 a pound.

Pocket mirror, "Stacey's Chocolates", 3 in. diameter.	$14
Chocolate box, tin, "Artstyle", 5 in. high.	$9
Box, tin, "Walter Baker Co./Breakfast Cocoa", slight stain.	$6.50
Tin, "Nelson's Breakfast Cocoa", 2-oz. size.	$14
Glass, soda, "Nestles Chocolate".	$18
Chocolate box, tin, lidded, "Golden Days".	$7.50
Spoon, advertising, "Fern Brand Chocolate".	$20
Watch fob, celluloid, fine cond., "Sparrow's Chocolate".	$12.50
Display cupboard, "Baker's Chocolate", wood.	$95
Sign, streetcar, "Ganongs Chocolate", 10 x 20 in., 1926.	$27
Sign, "Bakers Cocoa", tin, lithographed, large.	$350
Container, tin, "Monarch Cocoa", store-sized.	$15
Pocket mirror, "Hall's Chocolates".	$18
Sign, "Johnston's Chocolates", black and gold, fine cond.	$85
Puzzle, "Huyler's Cocoa", late 1800's.	$26
Tray, oval, "Baker's Chocolates", products shown.	$45
Box, dovetailed corners, "Baker's Chocolate", 1-lb. size.	$20
Pocket mirror, "Hershey Company", good glass and print.	$40
Sign, "Kayo/It's *Real* Chocolate", tin, 14 x 28 in., 1930's, rare.	$110
Tin, "Monarch Cocoa", small.	$10

Cigarettes

Cigarettes are small cigars, except that the tobacco is finely cut and the roll wrapped in thin paper. They were smoked more in the West, especially roll-your-own, in the late 1800's. Their use was not widely accepted in the East until the early 1900's, for cigarettes were thought rather "dandyfied", more a city habit. There were many

undred early makers, a few of which still exist. Signs, advertisements
nd early packages of all kinds are sought-after items.

Container, tin, "Cavalier Cigarettes", fine condition	$12
Cigarette package, "La Calpense/Gibralter", orig. contents.	$5
Cigarette tin, "Chesterfield", flat box, near-mint.	$7
Sample case, cigarettes, blue glass, quite rare.	$90
Thermometer, "Chesterfield Cigarettes", raised pack.	$30
Sign, "Piedmont Cigarettes", porcelian, two-sided, 13 in. square.	$60
Sign, framed cardboard, "Raleigh Cigarettes", dressed-up couple, 13 x 19 inches.	$25
Poster, "Turkey Red Cigarettes", wood frame.	$115
Puzzle, advertising, "Turkish Trophies Cigarettes", jigsaw.	$19
Match dispenser, "Kool Cigarettes", good condition.	$30
Sign, "Camel Cigarettes", cardboard, pretty blonde, 11 x 20 inches.	$15
Container, round, "Chesterfield Cigarettes", tin.	$12
Sign, "Master Mason Cigarettes", picturing girl.	$38
Cigarette tin, "Dill's Best", excellent condition.	$14
Sign, "Omar Cigarettes/20 for 15¢", 8 x 14 inches.	$45
Cigarette container, "Egyptian Deities", contents, 1920's.	$9

Coffee

There are many coffee-related collectibles, all dealing in some
way with the roasted beans of the coffee tree, genus *Coffea*. At an
early time in this country, tea or chocolate were the preferred social
drinks, especially in the upper classes, until replaced by this dark,
stimulating brew. There were many hundred early coffee brand
distributors, and some collectors select out-of-business names for their
field. Coffee-related items include ads., trade-cards, containers, bins,
grinders, giveaways or samples, plus utensils of all types.

Token, wood, "Sambo's Free Coffee".	$1.50
Tin, "Home Brand Coffee", 1-lb. size.	$5
Sign, "Arbuckles Coffee", tin, 9 in. high.	$40
Container, tin, "Wishbone Coffee", 5-lb. size.	$30
Tin, "Cheerio Coffee", bird litho., 1-lb. size.	$32
Can, pasteboard, "Eagle Coffee", fine condition.	$4
Container, tin, "Bours Higrade Coffee".	$9
Corkscrew, "Forbes Coffee", twist-type.	$10
Sign, "McLaughlin's Coffee", ca. 1900.	$55

Tin container, ½ x 3¼ x 3¾ in., "Watkins
Laxative Wafers /They do not Gripe", fine
lettering front and back, blue background.
$5

Lar Hothem collection

Store sign, large, advertising
"Satin Skin Cream", left, and
Powder, right. Lithographed
heavy paper, superb colors,
"Albert F. Wood, M'F'R /
Copyright 1903, mint condition.
Value is for both sign and frame.
$125

Photo courtesy Dan Poore, Ft.
Wayne, Indiana

Recipe booklet, "Cream of Rice", 4⅜ x 5
inches, printed shortly after 1921.
$3.25

Private collection

Face-mask, papier-mache, "San Marto Coffee". $11
Tin, "Parker House Coffee", 1-lb. size, contents, good. $18
Can, "Woolson's Vienna Coffee", 3-lb. size. $38
Grinder, home, "My-T-Good Coffee", ca. 1905. $40
Tin, "French Brand Coffee/Cincinnati", 1-lb. size. $17
Pail, "McLaughlin's Coffee", 5-lb. size. $55
Container, tin, "Macintosh's Coffee", very fine condition. $80
Match safe, "Bell Coffee", sheet brass. $19
Tin, small, "Glendora Coffee", good litho. label. $22
Container, "McLaughlin Coffee", 5-lb., good lettering. $60
Can, "Peak Coffee", 1-lb. size. $14
Bank, tin, "Red Circle Coffee", 1-lb. size. $17.50
Store jar, "Old Judge Coffee", glass, lidded. $18
Information cards, set of 50, all present, "Drink Lion
    Coffee". $38
Coffee grinder, "Crystal/Arcade", wall-hanging type. $95

Store/Saloon cash register, 15½ in. square, 22 in. high, all solid brass, with 25 keys (to $5.00). Very ornate scrollwork, model "The Total Adder", SN 45081. In working condition, complete with "Purchase" sign, label dates 1879 to 1891. Note, drawer pull is a caricature of the founder of NCR. Present, original bill of sale, July 8, 1891 signed "John Patterson/National Cash Register/Dayton, Ohio." Near mint condition.   (Scarce)

Courtesy Dan Poore, Fort Wayne, Indiana

Cash box, 17 in. wide, 19 in. deep, 9 in. high, tiger stripe dovetailed oak, brass trim and inkwell. It has five-key combination buttons for opening drawer and windowed paper slot for recording sales. Model, "No. 45", SN 701586. Slant top lifts to reveal original instructions, "The Autographic". Original bill of sale, "G. Schmidt Store/Fort Wayne, Indiana 1909/(signed) John Patterson, Pres., National Cash Register Co."—In complete working state, near mint condition. $750

Courtesy Dan Poore, Fort Wayne, Indiana

Store wall clock, ''Vanner & Prest's'', 4 in. deep, 31 in. high. Oak and papier mache construction, double-face Ionic wall regulator, key wind, 8-day pendulum movement, time only. Made by ''Baird Clock Co./Plattsburg, New York'', original label inside with instructions, dark red paint with silver lettering on case. Top door, ''Molliscorium'' harness oil, bottom door, ''Compo Embrocation'', liniment for humans. Excellent condition, ca. 1895. $1000

Courtesy Dan Poore, Fort Wayne, Indiana

Straw holder, 5 in. diameter, 10 in. high, heavy cut glass with folding brass top. Enameled both sides, ''Drink Grape Smash'' in raised letters while cluster of grapes holds company initials, a combined entertwined ''J'' & ''C''. Very fine condition, ca. 1900.   (Scarce)

Courtesy Dan Poore, Fort Wayne, Indiana

Store milk dispenser, 44 in. high, 31 in. wide, 24 in. deep, of 1¼ in. oak and curly maple. Construction, tongue and groove with dowel pins, ornate brass hardware, brass spigots. Rear hinged lift-top reveals two 20-gal. tin milk containers, ice-cooled; brass covered, side air vents. Side windowed spigots for drawing milk into pails, center spigot for ice water. Lower door reveals ice catch/drain pan. Brass label: ''Mosley's Occident Creamery/Patented Aug. 31, 1886/Mfg'd By Mosley & Pritchard, Clinton, Iowa''. Very fine condition. $2250
Figurine, ''Dutch Boy Paint'', 16 in. papier mache. $150
Figurine, ''Watta Pop Suckers—1¢'', plaster of paris, bulldog, 10 in. high. $100

Courtesy Dan Poore, Fort Wayne, Indiana

Cracker barrel, 17 in. diameter, 28 in. high, oak stave and wood band construction. Top label is original, "Montpelier Crackers & Confectionary/Montpelier, Vermont". Excellent condition, and ca. 1900. $325

Courtesy Dan Poore, Fort Wayne, Indiana

Baking powder barrel, 18 in. diameter, 26 in. high. Heavy paper (composition) construction, wooden band, advertising both sides "CALUMET— The World's Greatest Baking Powder". Excellent condition, ca. 1900. $295

Courtesy Dan Poore, Fort Wayne, Indiana

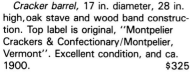

Advertising flashlight, "Burgess Battery Company", 7 in. long, fine cond., called a "Flashlight Substitution". $12

Courtesy Fairfield Antiques, Lancaster, Ohio

Stoneware crocks, original wire bales and lids, large specimens 9¼ in. high. Croc at right marked ''Cruikshank Bros. Co./Preserves, Jellies, Fruit Butters...''.

Left $4
Right $5
Center $2

Private collection

Coffee grinder, home size, dovetailed corners, faded label, 13 in. overall height. Condition, fine. $85

Private collection

Cream/egg whipper, tin, japanned wood handle, ''Fries'', 9½ in. high, fine condition. $50

Private collection

Store box, ''Steam Bakery/ Crackers, Cakes and Biscuits'', another perfect-condition label inside lid. Slat wood construction, box 10″14×22¾ inches. $55

Private collection

Candy dispenser, maker unknown, 15 in. diameter, 34 in. high, hand-made solid copper dovetailed tank with dome top. Pedestal 30 in. diameter is of spun copper. Ten pull drawers, brass labels above drawers. Very fine condition, ca. 1870. (Rare)

    Spittoon, solid brass, 16 in. high. $125

    Syrup dispenser, "Drink Green River" on both sides, with brass spigot. $325

Courtesy Dan Poore, Fort Wayne, Indiana

Counter-top coffee mill, 17-in. ameter wheels, 32 in. high, ast-iron. All original. Gold embossed "Elgin National Coffee ill/Woodruff & Edwards Co., gin, Illinois". Near mint condion, ca. 1890. $850

urtesy Dan Poore, Fort ayne, Indiana

    Counter coffee mill, "Elgin /National", some gold trim paint remaining, 27 in. high. Note: Wood handle is a replacement and top finial is missing. $225

Private collection

Store parlor stove, hard-coal baseburner, 72 in. high, 32 in. square, cast iron. It has 12 doors with 96 isenglass panels, ornate nickle top and trim, brass finial. Working condition, with all tools. Front, "Globe No. 115"; back, "Globe Stove Works, Kokomo, Indiana". Very fine condition, ca. 1895. (Rare)

Courtesy Dan Poore, Fort Wayne, Indiana

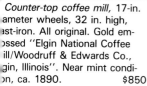

Store sign, 19 in. wide, 40 in. high, original wooden frame, ''Mecca Cigarettes''. Heavy poster print, beautiful woman in blue, signed ''F. Earl Christy/1912''. Excellent condition. $375

Courtesy Dan Poore, Fort Wayne, Indiana

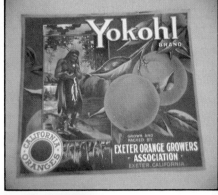

Fruit-crate label, mint cond., very colorful, 10×11 inches. $10

Private collection

Fruit-crate labels, various brands, average 9×10 size (inches), mint conditions. Value range, each, $6—$9

Private collection

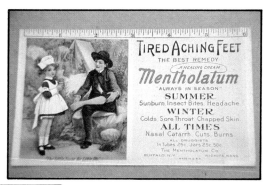

Trade-card "Mentho-latum/A Healing Cream/ Always in Season", 6-in. measure at top, thin card-board. $6
Private collection

Advertisement, "Barker's Nerve & Bone Liniment", 6¼ × 7 inches. Testimonial on back: "I could hardly stand up in the morning on account of my back being so weak... Today my back is as strong as ever." $5
Private collection

Trade card. "Pure Bone Fertilizers/The Return From The Insect Fair", bright, 3×5¼ inches. $4.50
Hothem collection

Nut jar, ''Planters/Chocolate Covered Filberts'', 7 oz. size, 4⅞ in. high, mint cond., dated 1944. $13
Private collection

Figural cookbooklet, ''Richard Hellmann's Mayonnaise''; 5½ in. high. Product recipes, by Niagara Litho. Co., unusual, 1920's. $13
Private collection

Store tin, ''Carbolized Mutton Tallow'', 1½ oz. size, 3 in. long, mint cond. $4.50
Private collection

Typewriter ribbon containers, tin, 2¼ in. square. Left, ''Kee-Lox Brand...Rochester, N.Y.'', fairly scarce, $6. Right, ''Remington/Paragon Non-filling Ribbon/Remington Typewriter Co.'', $5.
Private collection

Spice containers, center examples 3¼ in. high. Value range is, each, $1.50—$3.
Private collection

Sign, framed, half-price offer for "charming sleeping doll", made by Voigt's Flour Products.

$22

Lar Hothem photo

Trade-card, soap, 2½ x 4 in., "Use Pyle's Pearline / With Pearline a delicate woman can do a large wash. You do not have to rub yourself and your clothes to pieces. You do not have to inhale fetid steam...".

$2.50

Private collection

Coffee grinder, tin, "Star", 3-lb. size.	$22
Tin, rectangular, "Blanke's Happy Thoughts Coffee".	$49
Container, glass, "Old Judge Coffee", metal lid.	$14
Store container, tin "Durand & Kaster Coffee", litho label.	$80
Container, tin, "Red Wolf Coffee", 1-lb. size.	$26
Container, tin, lidded, "Mt. Cross Coffee".	$32.50
Tin, "After Glow Coffee", 4-lb. size.	$20
Puzzle, "Folger's Coffee", pastboard can, mint.	$18
Tin, "Golden Wedding Coffee", 3-lb. size, fine.	$26

Containers

Containers of all kinds are a very large store collecting field. These are of many materials, cardboard to metal to wood; those with product names and advertising are preferred over those that are plain. Value is enhanced if labels or lettering on a tin container are in fine condition, and the piece is rust-free and with few or no dents in the metal or stains on the paper. Generally, older containers are wood, more recent, cardboard or tin. Unfortunately, some of the old wood-staved containers were once heavily varnished or painted, obscuring the original lettering.

Stoneware pot, "Yale Mustard", pint-size.	$26
Box, "Garland Gloss Starch", 11 in. long.	$20

Box, wood, "Yeast Foam", lithographed print. $14
Jar, "Squirrel Peanuts", scarce brand. $30
Container, "Morton Bros.", tin, ca. 1880. $17
Container, "Bunnies Salted Peanuts", 10-lb. store size. $195
Box, cardboard, "Whitex Wonder Bluing". $4.50
Container, barrel, tin, "Calumet Baking Powder". $95
Box, wood, "Gloucester Style Codfish", 2 x 4 x 6 inches. $7
Container, "T. C. Baking Powder", 25 oz. size. $9.50
Tin, "Vigorator Tonic", some wear, 5 x 9 in., 1905. $36
Box, cardboard, "Ferguson's No-Wilt", empty. $6
Container, "Desert Sweet Dates", tin, large. $16.50

"Tote" Soda label, 4¼ in. wide, ca. 1930, mint.

Item courtesy Tom Mitchell, Canada

$1.25

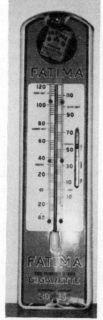

Scarce store item, early tin can for whale-oil, hand-soldered seams, screw top, 6 in. high. Marked, "Sperm Oil / ⅛ Gal.".

$45
Hothem collection

Thermometer, "Fatima Cigarettes", yellow and white porcelain. Large piece is 27 in. high, dated 1917.

$125
Courtesy Robert A. Hodge, Candler, North Carolina

Recipe booklet, "Lydia E. Pinkham's Medicine Company", 4½ x 7 in., 32 pages, ca. 1930, mint condition.

$4

Private collection

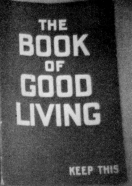

Recipe booklet, "Original Vinol / A Modern Tonic/Builds You Up"; 4½ x 6½ inches, 24 pages.

$4

Private collection

Recipe booklet, for "Certo Sure-jell", printed 1924, 6¼ in. high, 24 pages.

$3

Private collection

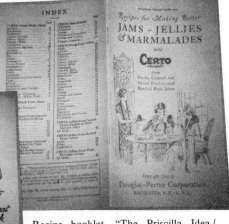

Recipe booklet, "The Priscilla Idea / Priscilla Prepared Products", 16 pages, 3⅜ x 6¼ in., ca. WW-I era.

$2.50

Private collection

Puzzle card, front, "The White Sewing Machine, 2¾ x 4½ in., ca 1890's. The viewer must locate eleven different hidden animals.

$2.75

Trade-card, front, Van Houten's Cocoa, 4¼ x 6½ in., bright, sharp colors.

$4.50

Private collection

Trade-card, "Davis Vertical Feed Sewing Machine / Fac-Simile of Embroidery", 3¼ x 5½ in., good color.

$3

Private collection

Box, wood, "Non-Such Mother's Mincemeat", 16 in. wide. $21
Container, tin, "Quaker Oats", 5½ in. high, unusual. $45
Tin, "Sante's Cottage Cheese", bright. $8.50
Container, tin, "Loose Wiles Biscuit Co.", octagonal. $19

Cracker box, tin, "Daintie Soda/White House Brand." $40

Tin, "Sunshine Biscuits", 3-lb. size, hinged top. $14

Store counter jar, "Tom's Peanuts". $21

Box, "Salerno Biscuit Pretzels", pasteboard. $22

Pail, wood-stave, handled, "Cruickshank's Apple Butter",
    1-gal. size. $43

Container, medium-size, "Fairy Drops", rare. $100

Box, wooden, "Carter's Blue Household Ink". $13

Motor oil can, "White Star", 1-gal., good condition. $9

Container, tin, "Seward Salmon", good label. $17

Box, dovetailed, "Jello", red lettering. $25

Container, "Planter's Peanuts", tin, 10-lb. size. $48

Tin, "United Biscuit Company", good litho., ca. 1915. $33

Container, tin, "Buffalo Brand Nuts", large size. $95

Store tin, "Malt Biscuit", lidded, blue, 12 in. square. $12

Store-box, "Elf Oats", wood, 3-lb. size. $15

Box, "Heinz Tomato Soup", dovetailed, 12 x 12 x 22 in. $60

Tin, "Crescent Crackers", 8½ in. high, good condition. $24

Can, wood, "Booth Oysters". $30

Jar, lidded, "Burma Shave", fine condition. $16

Tin, "Mica Axle Grease", 1-lb. size. $7

Container, "Maryland Beauty Oysters", tin. $28

Box, dovetailed corners, "Calapack Fruits". $8

Box, dovetailed, "DuPont Dynamite", 12 in. wide. $13

Box, "Yeast Foam", dovetailed, wood. $9

Biscuit box, "Austin Young & Co.", inside/outside labels. $45

Container, glass front, tin, "Stroh's Pretzels", square. $35

Box, cardboard, "Slidewell Soft Collars", three remaining. $12

Tin, "Edgemont Crackers", lid, litho., ca. 1924. $18

Tin, biscuit, "Loose-Wiles", octagonal. $27

Powder can, "DuPont", 1-lb. size. $12

Baking powder can, "Clabber Girl", 10-oz. size. $7

Flour

    Flour was one necessity that simply could not be home-made, since it required enormous and expensive equipment to crush grain to a fine powder. In early years, mills sprang up along good streams, and it was not uncommon for a person to make a journey of several days to the flour-mill. In the mid and late 1800's, brand names developed, and with better transportation, bags of flour were shipped

·M·O·K·A·S·K·A·

IS THE best roasted coffee ever sold in a one-pound
package. Many dealers won't sell it because they
can make more profit out of poorer coffees that
they buy for less money.

AN·ALBUM·FREE

FOR THIRTY OF OUR WRAPPERS.

Cut out the hands and triangle from thirty of our wrappers and send to us with sixteen cents for postage
and we will mail you

→ A Large Forty-Page Scrap-Album ←
to paste your pictures in.

Handsome and elegantly assorted Picture-Cards will be
found in all packages of

Mokaska Coffee.

Ask your Aunties, Cousins and Neighbors to
—BUY—

MOKASKA COFFEE

and save the wrappers for you.

Mokaska · Manufacturing
Company,
ST. JOSEPH, · · · MO.

Premium card, "Mokaska Coffee /Is the best roasted coffee ever sold in a one-pound package", 3¾ x 5 inches. Some staining.

$2.50

Private collection

Store-related items. Left, token good for two free bars of Crystal White laundry soap when three are purchased, 1½ in. across.

$1

Right, Pulver's Cocoa coupon that came in 10-cent can, entitles buyer to a free pack of chewing gum.

$0.50

Bottom, Philips advertising pocketknife, about mint, two-bladed, brass-lined, 3 in. long

$15

Private collection

Trade cut-out, 3¼ in. high, "Lion Coffee / No. 2 Old Mother Hubbard" (series), base missing for standup.

$1

Private collection

82

to country stores. (A mill operated in the mid-1800's not 50 yards from where this is being typed, and made "Lily Of The Valley" brands.) Flour mills operated wherever there was sufficient water-power.

Ad., "Pride Of Rockies Flour", string-hung, cardboard, 5 x 10 in., 1930's.	$5
Sign, tin, "Polar Flour", 13 in. high.	$55
Box, "Mother Hubbard Flour", 12½-lb. size, unusual.	$34
Thimble, advertising, "New Jersey Flour".	$9.50
Flour sack, cotton, "Mountain Pride Corn Meal".	$3
Sack, cotton, "Self Action Flour", 9 in. high.	$4
Watch fob, advertising, "Polar Bear Flour".	$42

Watch Fobs

Fobs, the ribbon or chain used to secure a pocket watch to the fob pocket, often carried ornate objects like seals or fraternal emblems. This was a fine place for advertising on a small scale, since the user periodically checked the time and noted the ad.'s message. Also, since the fob ornament usually hung outside the coat or vest, it could also be seen by others. Since people of means and taste carried fancy pocket watches, this would have been taken as product endorsement.

Watch fob, "Simon Pure Lard", mint condition.	$42
Watch fob, "Lone Star Cement", extra-fine cond.	$30
Watch fob, "Post Toasties", box-shaped.	$33
Key fob, "Use Lee Brooms", metal.	$27
Watch fob, "Poll Parrot Shoes", rare.	$65
Watch fob, "Lava Soap", fine condition.	$25
Watch fob, "Chamberlain Baking Powder".	$19

Chewing Gum

Chewing gum is named after a tree-sap or gum, and a principle ingredient is the coagulated juice of the sapodilla tree. In sticks or "gum-drops", the sap was flavored and sweetened, sold for both a pleasurable candy or breath-freshener. "Bubble" gum, a late addition to store stock, had ingredients that smoothed the texture and held air in balloon-like creations. Gum has always been promoted as a teeth-cleanser and tension-reliever.

Sign, tin, "Wrigley's Gum", 13 in. long.	$115
Sign, tin, "Black Jack Chewing Gum".	$42.50

Pocket box, "Gold Tip Peppermint Gum", cigarette
    shapes. $7
Sign, cardboard, "Beech-Nut Gum", couple shown smoking,
    10 x 20 inches. $16
Ad., paper, "California Fruit Chewing Gum", large size. $98
Ad., cardboard, "Long Chew 1¢ Gum", 4½ x 8 in.,
    1910's. $24
Sign, "Wrigleys Chewing Gum", colorful, 1920's. $95
Sign, tin, "O Boy Gum", large. $105
Sign, tin, "Chew Walla Walla Gum", 9¼ x 18½ inches. $60

Ice Cream

Ice cream, frozen custard, iced milk — by whatever name, ice cream has long been an American treat. Most mixtures contain 10 to 14 percent butterfat, over 10 percent nonfat milk solids, some 15 percent sugar, plus flavors and colors. Ice cream has been served as cones, bars, sodas, shakes and sundaes. The last were once thought of as too good to be eaten on Sunday, so the spelling was changed. And, for many years, the hand-cranked home ice cream maker was a family necessity.

Sign, "Marrows Ice Cream", hanging, porcelain faces. $95
Sign, "Crown Quality Ice Cream", tin, good condition. $85
Clicker, tin, "Sealtest Ice Cream", toy. $7
Tray, oval, "Bissantz Ice Cream", pretty girl, ca. 1900. $85
Ice cream scoop, brass bowl and body, hardwood handle. $38
Ad., "Bemis Ice Cream", cardboard, 10 x 14 in., 1920's. $20
Popgun, "Clover Ice Cream", litho. cylinder, ca. 1915. $15

Kitchen Aids

It is not difficult to understand why so many product makers had giveaways or premium objects useful in the kitchen. For years, this was the social center of the home, and all family members came in contact with the advertisements. The housewife was surrounded with helpful little items that not only did their special work, but hinted that one product was a good deal better than all others. It was a permanent form of "choose me".

Potato/fruit peeler, "Morton Salt". $17
Bottle opener, iron, "Williams Shaving Soap". $6

Doughnut cutter, "Rumford Baking Powder", mint. $9

Cookbook, "Bunte Cocoa", clean, 1918. $11

Cookbook, "Golden Rule Food Products", 1916. $5

Shaker, "McCormick & Co. Spices", glass. $11

Ceramic beater, blue on grey, "Wesson Oil". $70

Cake turner, "S & H Green Stamps/Discount", ca. 1910. $8

Potholder, "Glenwood Ranges And Heaters/Hot Iron Holder". $4

Cookie cutter, "Davis Baking Powder", scarce. $7

Mug, advertising, "Mr. Peanut". $4.25

Cup, "Ft. Bedford Peanut Butter". $60

Flour-sifter, "Majestic Range". $17

Cup, "Horlicks", ceramic. $10

Measure, "Miss Princine Baking Powder", tin. $14

Mixing bowl, "Diamond Crystal Shaker Salt", 7¾ in. dia. $19

Salt and pepper shakers, Campbell Kids. $24

Cook booklet, "Occident Flour / Tested Recipes", ca. 1910. $2.50

Knife sharpener, "Bull Moose 5¢ Cigar / Skowhega, ME". $24

Recipe, giveaway, "French's Mustard". $7

Pamphlet, cookbook, "Cox's Gelatine Cookery", good. $4.50

Cookbook, "Dr. Sloan's Handy Hints" (maker of horse cure-alls), 1901. $5.50

Tea strainer, "Quick Action Range", tin. $9

Flour sifter, "Bromwell", tin. $4

Thermometer, stove-top, "Swans Down Flour", enameled. $8

Juice reamer, milk glass, "Sunkist". $9

Spatula, "Log Cabin", lithographed. $20

Egg separator, "South Bend Malleable Range", tin. $20

Phamphlet, "Calumet Baking Book", 1930's. $5

Measuring cup, "Kelloggs", green glass. $14

Pot-scraper, "Sharples Cream Separator". $30

Knife sharpener, "Pine Tree Farm Seeds". $27

Sifter, "Nesco Flour", wire and tin. $7.50

Cook booklet, "Dwight's Cow Brand Soda", 1895. $3.50

Spoon, metal, "Log Cabin" (syrup). $27

Cereal bowl, "Uneeda Biscuits", porcelain. $25

Grater, tin, "Fels Naptha Soap". $6

Jar, measuring, handle, 1880, product name. $17.50

Spoon, celluloid, "French's Mustard". $2.50

Salesman's samples, in original carrying case, for the Royal Baking Powder Company. It contains two bottles of Cream of Tartar (one crystal, one powdered) and a bottle of Crude Argol.

$50

Lar Hothem photo

Bottle, stoppered, partial contents, "Certified Food Color, Knapp Extracts".

$2.50

Private collection

Medicinal bottle, "Souders Elegant Flavoring Extracts", 5 in. high, embossed printing.

$4

Private collection

Bottle, "3-in-One Oil Co.", pale green, cork top, mint condition, 3¾ in. high. According to the company (Boyle-Midway /Division of American Home Products) bottles like this were made only between 1905-1910. Screw-top glass bottles appeared in 1910.

$6

Private collection

Cookie cutter, tin, "Davis Baking Powder", good.	$9
Biscuit or cookie cutter, "Rumford".	$12
Pitcher, child-size, "Post Cereals Measured Creamer".	$12
Towel holder, "Aunt Jemima", wood.	$25
Rolling pin, "F. & H. / Gen. Merchandise.", crockery.	$155
Soap shaver, "Fels Naptha", tin.	$7
Bottle opener, cast-iron, "Davis Paints".	$3
Donut cutter, "Cottonlene For All Frying And Shortening".	$10
Recipe book, "Cow Brand Baking Soda", 1933.	$3
Salt and pepper shakers, "Pillsbury".	$18
Measure, pint size, "Kelloggs", pink depware.	$27
Scoop, tin, "Buy Royal Patent Flour", 5 in. long.	$15

Lard

This was the white rendered fat of hogs, sold solid or semi-solid in the store. It gives us the word "larder", a space where meat was kept. Lard was an important product, because it was necessary for so many other foods. In a day without corn-oil or sunflower oil, it was the only substance for deep-frying and "shortening" for baking.

Container, "Squire & Co. Lard", 8-lb. size.	$13
Pail, lidded, "Double-D Brand Lard", 8-lb. size.	$11
Tub, staved, "Silver Leaf Lard", 105-lb., wood top.	$55
Tin, lard, "Morrell's Snow Cap", 8-lb. size.	$28
Bucket, "American Sunrise Lard", tin, 25-lb. size.	$40
Tin, "Goodwill Pure Lard", litho. of pig, lidded.	$70
Pail, "Murphy's Lard", tin, 3 in. diameter.	$18
Pail, "Swift's Silver Leaf Lard", bale handle.	$55

Match-Holders

Matches were a great improvement over earlier ways of fire-starting, flint-and-steel, the coals-container, the burning-glass. Large, old-fashioned kitchen matches were the strike-anywhere type, with heads that combined a friction starter plus sustainer chemical. Since matches were used frequently, holders were kept in a prominent place so it made sense to place advertising on them.

Match-holder, "Sharples Cream Separator".	$95
Match-safe, "Knapsack Matches", tin.	$11
Match-safe, "Gillette", chrome.	$14

Match-holder, "Garland Stoves", cast-iron, rust free. $75

Match-holder, frog shape, "Garland Stoves", cast-iron. $80

Match-safe, "Sharples Cream Separator Works". $40

Match-holder, hanging, "Bliss Native Herbs", tin. $49

Medicinal

In store days, medicines were more purchased than prescribed and most "Doctors" gave that designation to themselves in products. A vast and wonderful array of products emerged, designed to cure everything from warts to wasting-away. With our current technology, these products seem most archaic, and they are collected with both interest and amusement. Some makers made great fortunes with their patent medicines.

Sign, "Horse and Dog Medicines", small, tin. $29

Box, "Chief 2 Moons" medicine, 9 in. high, ca. 1943. $5

Sign, tin, "Acco-Balm / For Colds & Burns", 5 x 8 in., 1920's. $12

Tin, medicine, "Salt Petre", 1 x 3 in., label, 1930's. $3.50

Cask, "Spirits of Turpentine", metal top. $30

Medicine, "Dr. Jackson's Neutralizing Cordial", bottle. $17

Calendar, "Mrs. Dinsmore's Balsam", mother and child, 1901. $40

Urn, "Trixy Specific Exhalant / Concord, NH". $10

Tin, "Horehound Cough Drops", small. $18

Tin, "Dr. Scott's Electric Foot Salve", round, lidded. $7

Bottle, "Dr. Hostetters Stomach Bitters", amber. $12

Box, cardboard, "Penetrol Cold Capsules". $3

Sample, "Sure Relief", 2 in. diameter, 1910's. $3.50

Tin, "Mothersill's Seasick Remedy", lidded. $3

Ad., "Baby's Pineapple Honey" (worm medicine), 1907. $19

Sign, tin, "Willard's Stomach Treatment", 18 in. long. $36

Tin, "Rawleigh Ointment", small (sample) size. $4

Sign, "Dr. Miles Nervine", cardboard under glass, 14 x 26 inches. $195

Bottle, "Blood Vitalizer", embossed, 5½ in. high. $10

Sign, "Dr. Meyer's Foot Soap", cardboard, hands with soap bars, 7 x 10 inches. $9

Box, cardboard, "Corbett's Shaker Medicated Losenge", ca. 1880. $26

Brochure, cardboard, "Shaker Medicinal Spring Water". $55

Top, Ad. booklet, 64 pages, 1890, "Crocker Honest Fertilizers", showing poor farmer not using products.

$6

Bottom, Crocker fertilizer booklet, 1890, 3¾ x 6½ in., showing wealthy farmer after using ad. products.
Private collection

Tin, "Wonder Salve", cure-all, 2 in. diameter, 1910's.	$3
Sign, "Beef and Iron Restorative Tonic", tinned iron.	$160
Sign, tin, "Kemps Balsam", girl taking cough medicine.	$155
Sign, "Glover's Dog Remedies", 15½ in. diameter.	$200
Bitters, "Atwoods Jaundice", 6 in. high.	$7

Trade-card picturing Windsor Castle, 100 cards in series. On back, "Jersey Coffee/ Dayton Spice Mills Co.", 3 x 4 inches.

$1.25

Trade-card, 3½ x 5½ in., "Everybody drink Sarica Coffee", four cats parading, back blank, edge-tip missing.

$3.25

Private collection

Diamond Dye trade-card, front, 3½ x 5 inches, "Unequaled for making Ink, or for coloring any article any color", schoolyard scene.

$5

Private collection

Peanut Butter

Peanut butter is still a sandwich mainstay, this breaded snack named after the 4th Earl of Sandwich who had fast food brought to his gaming table. It is a thick paste made from roasted and ground peanuts, and many early brands existed. In the store, peanut butter first came in staved pails, with peanut oil floating on top, and it was dispensed into the buyer's container. Eventually it was packaged in pails which the customer took with them.

Peanut butter pail, "Sunny Boy", unusual, excellent condition.	$48
Pail, tin, "Sultana Peanut Butter".	$22
Container, peanut butter, "Peter Rabbit", lithographed.	$90
Pail, "Buffalo Brand Peanut Butter", 1-lb. size.	$50
Container, tin, "Sultana Peanut Butter", with lid.	$30
Pail, "Sultana Peach Peanut Butter", 1-lb., lidded.	$37
Container, "Sunny Boy Peanut Butter", 1-lb. size.	$85
Pail, "Red Seal Brand Peanut Butter", 1-lb. size.	$40
Pail, "Shedd's Peanut Butter", bail handle.	$13.50

Pocket Mirrors

These mirrors are yet another small item that advertisers selected to reflect their product. The mirrors were used by adults for personal grooming and children for play and "signaling" one another. Collectors seek those with unusual ads. on the backs, or those for little-known products.

Pocket mirror, "Red Seal Lye".	$21
Pocket mirror, "Angelus Marshmellows", two cupids with confection.	$80
Pocket mirror, "Diamond Saw Stamping Works", 2 in. diameter.	$17
Pocket mirror, "Mr. Peanut", 1930's.	$12
Pocket mirror, "Angelus Marshmellows", plain.	$35
Pocket mirror, celluloid, "Washington Crisps Cereal".	$13

Rag Dolls

Rag dolls with advertising have been offered as collectibles for some years, and they are still in favor. These were frequently product premiums, and were very popular with children. The dolls were hard-used, and not many exist in fine condition, adding a scarcity

Thermometer, advertising, 15 in. high: "Grapette/ Grape Soda".

$14

factor. Those with bright and distinct lettering, and those that have not been laundered out of shape, receive the most attention.

Rag doll, "Kellogg's Papa Bear", 13 in. high.	$40
Rag doll, "Aunt Jemima", with plate of hotcakes.	$45
Rag doll, "Mr. Peanut", Planters Peanuts, 20 in. high.	$35
Rag doll, "Cream of Wheat", mint condition.	$85
Rag doll, "Jack Frost", (sugar), 18 in. high.	$30
Rag doll, "Snow King Baking Powder", 12 in. high.	$28

Salesman's Samples

Samples carried by salesmen or factory "reps" can be categorized in two ways. One is the object that, like stoves, furniture and farm equipment, took their place because the originals were too bulky or heavy to transport. Another was for the agent that represented the maker of a "line" of dozens of objects. Whether buckets or equipment, the sample case was filled with the small objects. A true salesman's sample was constructed to exact scale, and any moving parts must function like the original.

Salesman's sample, oak rocker, cane seat.	$60
Iron, "Mrs. Potts Irons", 3¾ in. long.	$20
Salesman's sample, "Majestic Furnace".	$175
Miniature horseshoe, sample, "Snowcleat".	$36
Sample briefcase, "W. D. Smith Co.", clothing.	$45
Sample, candy case, small sealed containers.	$75
Sample, brass kettle, 2¾ in. diameter.	$60

Sample, set of miniature tin cookie-cutters, early 1900's. $70
Sample, wooden wash-tub, "Relief Wringer", fine. $135

Samples

Another kind of sample was the product giveaway, a small container of goods that otherwise could be purchased in larger quantities. This was profitable two ways. The customer received something free, and the maker had coaxed someone to sample the product, with possible later sales. Small containers are in demand, paper, cardboard and metal, and very many brand-names exist.

Soap sample, "Lifebuoy". $9
Giveaway, "Calumet Baking Powder", 4-oz. packet. $6
Container, sample, "Glendora Coffee", tin. $23
Giveaway, "The Home Needle Case", ca. 1920. $6
Sample, "Condo Silver Polish", tin, lithographed. $3

Sewing

Sewing goods, like kitchen aids, were usually handled often, so had ads. for many products. Even in the late 1800's, some skilled seamstresses were not convinced that the machine was superior to hand-sewing. Singer machines became highly popular because the thread hole was near the needle tip, which proved highly successful. At the time, competing machines had holes near the needle's base.

Sewing tape, "Our Native Herbs", 36 in. long. $10
Scissors sharpener, "Niagara #9", iron. $4
Hem-measurer, "Feen-A-Mint", cast-iron, square base. $24
Needle container, wood, "Boye Needle Co.". $2
Booklet, children's "Clark's O.N.T. / Rhymes For All
     Times". $10
Sewing tape, "Boot 'n' Shoe Workers Union", ca. 1900. $18.50
Tape measure, "Dixie Lye", like-new. $30
Needle container, "Old Ben Coal", paper. $2.50
Pan, "Wheeler & Wilson Sewing Machines". $5

Shoes

Once store buyers recognized that left- and right-shaped shoes were more comfortable, and small factories became more efficient than individual cobblers, many hundred shoe-makers entered the market. They advertised on many objects, but toys were a favorite.

This was because growing children required shoes more often than adults, and a child could influence the parents' choice of footwear. Too, the toys were cheap to manufacture. Objects for adults were included as well, since they were the actual buyers.

Shoe-horn, iron, "Freeman Shoes".	$2.25
Ruler, wood, "Johnson Shoes", good condition.	$2.50
Whistle, tin, "Red Goose Shoes", two-tone.	$7
Magic lantern slide, large, "Nettleton Shoes".	$8
Sign, tin, "Florsheim Shoes", 13 x 20 in., 1920's, scarce.	$56
Shoe-horn, tin, "Shinola".	$15
Popgun, "Newman's Shoes", 1930's premium, 7 in. long.	$4
Blotter, 4 x 7 in., "Ball Brand Shoes".	$2
Dictionary, child's "Peter's Weatherbird Shoes".	$5
Scale, "Friedman-Shelby Shoes", home-type.	$20
Clicker, tin, "Poll Parrot" (shoe-brand).	$4
Scissors, "Star Brand Shoes", in case.	$8
Notebook, lined paper, "Red Goose Shoes".	$6
Pocket mirror, "Buster Brown Shoes".	$29
Sign, "Red Goose Shoes", porcelain, neon, attractive.	$500
Ruler, wood, "Star Brand Shoes".	$5

Advertising cut-out, 4¼ in. high, "All us School Girls Wear Standard Screw Fastened Boots and Shoes / They are so Nice".

$3.5

Lar Hothem collection

Ad cards, 1⅞ in., "Arm and Hammer Brand/Great Blue Heron", no. 42 in a series of 60.

$1.25

Private collection

Pencil box, pencil shape, "Poll Parrot Shoes",
    lithographed. $26
Pocket mirror, "West Coast Shoe Company". $14
Holder, for pens and letters, "Diamond Brand Boots". $23
Bill-hook, "Red Goose Shoes", fine condition. $6
Button-hook, metal, "Walkover Shoes". $2
Clicker, tin, "Red Goose Shoes". $5

Signs

Signs are widely accepted as one of **the** store items, and they are a major collecting field. Outdoor signs were usually metal or of other durable materials, quite large to attract the attention of passersby. Indoor signs — stand-up, hanging and poster or wall — could be smaller and less durable. Outdoor signs drew interest to the establishment, while indoor signs stressed products sold there, or gave a special notice. There is a mixture of categories among some signs and advertisements, with collectors calling them either or both.

Sign, tin, "Old Dutch Cleanser", 14 in. wide. $28
Sign, tin, "Surge Milkers", 12 x 18 in., fine colors, 1940. $44
Sign, tin, "Illinois Watches / Always On Time", 12 x 18
    in., ca. 1910. $375

An assortment of jugs (small mouths, handles), a crock and a lidded pot. These were always general store stock and many were sold for home use.

                                      Each ... $7 - $12

Lar Hothem photo

Store-card, 3¾ x 4¾ in., done in various shades of green and black, unusual, attractive.

$3

Hothem collection

Story booklet, "Happy Hours in Picture Land / Mellin's Foods For Infants and Invalids", 4¾ x 5¾ inches. This booklet was distributed by "Clark & Colmery / Foreign and Domestic Grocers".

$5

Private collection

Sign, tin, "Colorite Dye", 12 in. long. $70

Sign, "Keystone Watch Case Company", tin. $300

Sign, paper, "Woo Chee Chong Import Co.", hanging, 21 x 31 inches. $35

Sign, "Putnam Dyes", 14 x 19 in., Revolutionary War scene. $85

Sign, "Heinz Sweet Pickles", approx. 19 in. wide. $175

Store sign, on tin, stock feeds, etc., 10 x 20 inches. $37

Sign, "Nabisco Biscuits", cardboard, 11½ in. wide. $60

Sign, "Sharples Tubular Cream Separators". $60

Sign, tin, "South Bend Watches", 10 x 30 in., 1920's. $75

Sign, "Powerlube Oil", porcelain, 20 x 28 in., color on both sides, 1920's. $300

Sign, "Denver Sandwich", 12 x 24 in., embossed, colorful, 1930's. $70

Sign, paper, hanging, "Rogers Paints / Varnishes". $50

Gasoline sign, "Shamrock Gasoline", porcelain, 12 in. square. $35

Sign, "Dr. Nutt Soda", embossed tin, 10 x 13 in., 1920's. $54

Sign, "Chief Paints", Indian, tin, some rust. $20

Sign, tin, "Post No Bills", 7 x 10 in., 1930's. $8

Sign, "Remington Tires", 32 in. wide, tin. $35

Sign, "Dutch Cleanser", porcelain, 22 x 33 inches. $225

Sign, porcelain, "Goodrich", large. $55

Sign, tin, "Star Belt Lacing", 13 x 19 in., 1909. $44

Sign, "Glesby's Feeds", embossed tin, 12 in. square,
    1940's. $16

Sign, "Cash Reward", tin, 7 x 12 in., 1940's. $14

Sign, "Corker Soda", 7 in. diameter, hanging, celluloid
    over tin. $18

Sign, tin, "Embro Corn", 11 x 13 in., colorful ear, 1940's. $23

Sign, "O-Cedar Polish", illustrating bottle. $35

Sign, "Drink Granite Rock Beverages", 9 x 19½ inches. $19

Sign, tin, "Congress Tires", ca. 1915. $275

Sign, "Fisk Tires", heavy paper, 28 x 48 inches. $85

Sign, tin, "Masterpiece Fertilizer", 14 x 20 in., orange and
    black, 1930's. $22

Sign, "Round Oak Stoves", cardboard, Indian head, 8 in.
    dia. $18

Sign, "Watch Repairing", framed paper under glass,
    3½ x 12 inches. $16

Sign, "Remington Arms", paper under glass, game chart,
    21 x 29 inches. $85

Sign, "Volcano Stove Polish", tin, bright. $155

Sign, "Singer Sewing Machine", glass, 6 x 14 in., 1940. $24

Soap

Like shoes, soap was another product that was far easier to purchase than make at home. Few families eventually cared to collect fat or tallow and wood-ashes for lye, and go through the long process of homemade soap-making. Manufacturers advertised in many ways, and the soap-box was a later store container. Factory-made soap tended to be "gentler" and smelled better. "Soap operas" are so-called because the early day-time serials on the radio were financed by soap companies.

Sign, cardboard, "Swan Soap", 7½ in. wide. $25

Pinback button, "Swift Company Wool Soap", fine. $16

Ad., "Little Fairies Bath Powder", 9 x 10 in., cardboard,
    1910's. $6

Calendar, "Fairy Soap", year 1900. $52.50

Box, "Cheerio Soap", full contents, 1920's. $7.50

Token, "Good For 1 Bar / Lava Soap". $3.50

Sign, "Lilac Rose Soap", 12 in. high.	$80
Pail, tin, "Just Soap", 1930's, orange and black.	$17
Tip tray, "Fairy Soap", little girl sitting on soap bar.	$40
Sign, "Fairy Soap", girl on product.	$135
Box, cardboard, "Gold Dust" washing powder, 6 in. high, ca. 1940.	$9
Ad., "Pure White Floating Fairy Soap", 22 x 23 inches.	$120
Print, "Babbitt's Soap", cardboard, 1880's.	$6
Tape measure, celluloid, "Colgate's Detergent".	$8
Ad., "Gouraud's Shampoo", 9 x 20 in., cardboard, 1920's.	$18

Soft Drinks

Soft (non-alcoholic) drinks have been popular for a long time; their common name, "pop", came from the explosive release of gas when the top was released. The basic "soda pop" (sodium carbonate) or "carbonated water" consisted of water, flavor, colorant and gas bottled under pressure. Early bottles had caps of round, marble-like seals, wired-on corks or ceramic stoppers. The more popular U.S. soft drinks have been fruit or berry flavors, plus "colas", which once contained an extract from kola nuts.

Fan, "Moxie", lady pictured, excellent condition, 1920's.	$50
Sign, "Mil-Kay Vitamin Drink", unusual.	$90
Blackboard, "R.C. Cola", red and white.	$30
Clicker, tin, "Smile" orange soda pop.	$7
Pitcher, miniature, "Schweppes Soda", brown glaze.	$20
Ad., cardboard, "Orange Bubble Soda", 7 x 7 in., 1920.	$6
Sign, "Moxie", 12 x 36 in., metal, large.	$395
Ad., "Sunspot Soda", colorful, 6 x 7 in., cardboard, 1940's.	$4
Mug, "Lash's Root Beer", ceramic, glazed.	$25
Sign, "Red Rock Cola", tin, 39 in., wide.	$75
Sign, tin, "Goldylock Birch Beer", 10 x 20 in., 1930's.	$14
Ad., "First Aid Orange Soda", cardboard, 10 x 13 in., 1920's.	$7
Coca Cola tray, springboard girl, 1939.	$55
Tumbler, glass, "Moxie".	$22
Sign, tin, "Vitalized Ginger Ale", girl surfing, 7 x 9 in., 1930's.	$75
Sign, "Lime Julep", embossed tin, 7 x 19 in., 1920.	$56
Watch fob, metal, "Chero-Cola".	$35

Mug, "Hires Root Beer", by Mettlach, 5 in. high. $140
Ad., "Martini Soda Pop / 5¢", cardboard, 10 x 15 in.,
    1910's. $10
Postcard, ca. 1939, Coca-Cola truck, yellow. $3.50
Coca-Cola lighter, miniature bottle, ca. 1946. $12
Sign, tin, "Howel's Root Beer", tin, bottle-shaped, 9 x 29
    inches. $45
Mug, "Dad's Root Beer", heavy clear embossed glass. $8
Thermometer, "Coke", bottle-shaped. $40
Poster, "Coca-Cola", "Our American Glass / No. 2",
    22 x 32 inches. $35
Sign, "Grape Ola", tin, basket of grapes, 15 x 20 inches. $35
Coca-Cola pencil sharpener, miniature bottle, metal. $18
Bottle, "Orange Crush", 24 oz. size. $50
Sign, porcelain, "Dr. Pepper", 10 x 27 inches. $125
Sign, "Hires Root Beer", tin, circular. $35
Sign, "Enjoy Kist Beverages / Take Home A Carton",
    18 in. wide. $40
Coca-Cola calendar, 1943, pictures W.A.C. $60
Coca-Cola sign, 10 in. diameter, tin, picturing bottle. $35
Sign, "Dr. Pepper", orange on white, tin. $57.50
Coca-Cola thermometer, two bottles, 1942, 7 x 15 inches. $75
Ad., "Cal Cola / 5¢", cardboard, 7½ x 12 in., 1910's. $8

———————— -

Sweeteners

Syrups of many kinds were once in the store. These ranged from all natural (wild honey) to the various processed examples of maple and cane syrups. All were thick, sweet, sticky liquids, each with its own special flavor. It took from 40 to 60 gallons of sap-water to make a good gallon of maple syrup. When short, in the home, a passable syrup was made from sugar and water.

Syrup tin, "Log Cabin". fine condition. $40
Tin, "Log Cabin Syrup", pint size, label. $22
Sign, "Uncle John's Syrup", lithographed outdoors picture. $34
Sign, "Uncle John's Syrup", paper, U.J. with oxen, 11 x
    21 inches. $17
Tin, "Penn Mar / 5 lbs. / Golden Syrup". $12
Syrup tin, "Log Cabin", gallon size, clean. $27
Container, "Saskatchewan Honey", wheatfield
    lithograph. $12.50

Bucket, "Pure Maple Sugar", orig. label, 6 in. diameter. $35

Tea

Tea was an important store item even in the 1700's, and the dried leaves of eastern Asian shrubs were major early trade items. Tea has added words to our language, like teaspoon, teacup, teakettle, Boston Tea Party. Tea came into the store in large shipping boxes, usually 100-lb. weights, but sometimes more or less. The contents were additionally packaged in a kind of foil to preserve leaf freshness.

Box, "Monarch Tea", 1-lb. size, unusual. $25
Creamer, "Lipton Tea", black china. $6
Pickle fork, "Jewel Tea", 8 in. long. $13
Cooler, "Tetley Iced Tea", brown and cream, spigot, lid. $70
Tea tin, "Chase & Sanborn's", half-pound size. $14
Box, "Jack Sprat Tea", 3 x 3 x 5 in., color, 1930's. $4
Plate, tin, "Union Pacific Tea Co.", 1907. $48
Postcard, "Lipton's Teas and Coffees", bright colors. $5
Container, tin, "Betsy Ross Tea", 10¢ size. $6.50

Thermometers

A "thermo-meter", as the name suggests, measured heat. Someone was always looking at the temperature, so these were fine places for an advertising message. Outdoor thermometers usually had a large wood or metal frame so that words could be read from a distance. The instruments were also relatively inexpensive to make, so they were an economical way to advertise. Collectors look for thermometers with unbroken glass, unrusted, good paint and clear lettering.

Thermometer, "Prestone Anti-Freeze", tin. $28
Thermometer, "L & M Cigarettes", raised pack design. $30
Thermometer, "B - 1 Soda", tin, 5 x 16 in., new in orig.
    box, 1940's. $36
Thermometer, "Pepsi", raised cap, yellow. $30
Thermometer, "RC Cola", only fair condition. $18
Thermometer, "Ex-Lax", good condition". $40
Thermometer, "Golden Leaf Flour", tin. $33
Thermometer, tin, "Motorola", about 3 ft. high. $75
Thermometer, "A Treat Beverages". $50
Thermometer, "Hires", 27 in. high. $45

Thermometer, "Carter's Inks", porcelain. $95
Thermometer, "Universal Batteries", quite early. $60

Tins

Tins large and small are classic store items. The containers are really very thin steel, coated with a layer of tin to prevent rusting and protect the contents. Tin "cannisters" became cans, and are still with us. Containers range in size from large store tins to tiny product samples. And there are enough varieties to keep most collectors happy — and ever on the lookout for that extra-fine and rare tin.

Box, tin, "Family Herb Tablets", 3 in. long. $5
Tin, "Monarch Tea", 6½ in. high. $15
Tin, "Dupont Smokeless Shotgun Powder", 8-oz. size, label. $19
Tin, "Little Buster Popcorn", elf depicted at fireplace. $10
Tin, small, "Calumet Baking Powder". $12
Tin, "Benner's Baking Powder". $9
Tin, "Buster Brown Mustard", fine condition. $95
Box, tin, "Sensible Tobacco". $12
Container, tin, "Daisy Fly Killer". $18
Tin, candy, "Sunbrite", blue. $27
Tin, "Bee Brand Insect Powder", small. $7
Tin, "Excelsor Metal Polish", 2½ in. high. $8
Pocket tin, "Union Leader Tobacco". $7
Tin, small, "Victor Needles", for Victrola. $30
Tin, "Planters Peanuts", 5-lb., rust-free. $40
Tin, "Red Top Axle Grease", good condition. $7
Tin, "DuPont Smokeless Shotgun Powder", ½ lb. size. $35
Tin, "Gordon's Potato Chips", 1-lb. size. $30
Sample tin, "Armand Powder", 1¾ in. diameter, 1920's. $8
Box, tin, "Mrs. MacGregor's Family Nail Box", 3½ in.
     wide. $18
Tin, "Monarch Mints", round, 1-lb. size. $13.50
Container, metal, "Sleep Eze". $3
Tin, "Riley's Toffee", good lithograph. $9
Container, tin, for violin rosin, partial label. $2.75
Tin, "DuPont Gunpowder", 2 x 4 x 6 in., 1930's. $30
Tin, "Peppets Laxative Tablets". $3
Tin, "Hercules Blasting Caps", near mint. $17
Box, tin, "Edison Mazda Lamps". $27
Container, tin, "Kellogg's All-Bran". $22.50

Bronze medal / good-luck piece, top drilled for suspension, by "Excelsior Shoe Co. / Shoes for boys". Piece is 1¼ in. diameter, dated July, 1910.

$12

Hothem collection

Container, tin, "Wizard Oil Liniment". $2.50
Container, tin, "Rosemary Coffee', 1-lb. size. $16

Tobacco

Probably, a number of early stores would have failed were it not for the fact that they carried the processed leaves of the plant genus *Nicotiana*. Originally from Central America, early explorers in the southern U.S. found American Indians smoking tubes of rolled tobacco, which the Mayan Indians called a sik'ar. Tobacco was traded to Europe and the colonies, and soon became a world-wide habit. Some called it "that noxious weed" while others claimed it had medicinal value. Early store humor had it that the cheapest tobacco smelled like "burning hoof parings".

Sign, "We Sell Star Tobacco", porcelain, 1½ ft. wide. $55
Tobacco tin, "North Pole Smoking Cut Tobacco", 6 in.
  high. $60
Cigarette tin, "Melachrino", flat. $8.50
Tobacco lunchbox, "Dixie Queen", extra-fine. $85
Jar, "Ohio Cigars", glass, wood lid. $13
Lunch-pail, "Tiger Tobacco", red and black stripes. $45
Tobacco tin, "Edgeworth Extra High Grade / Ready
  Rubbed". $9
Tobacco tin, "Dutch Masters Special Quality Cigars", 5½
  in. diameter. $21
Tobacco bag, "Solace Brand", 4 x 5 in., beautiful lady,
  1890's. $2
Ad., "Pig Tail Crooks 5¢ Cigar", cardboard, poster, 6 x 18
  in., 1920's. $7
Tobacco tin, "The Elm", litho of elm tree and village, a
  scarce item. $100
Package, small, "Snow Apple Tobacco". $3.50

Storage jar, glass, "Weyman's Snuff". $32
Ad., "Free Land Cigar / 10¢", cardboard, 3 x 15 in., 1920's. $7
Container, tin, "Dan Patch Cut Plug". $33
Ad., "Lord Baltimore Cigar", 7 x 13 in., bright colors, 1930's. $8
Tobacco tin, "American Navy", 3 x 4½ x 6½ inches. $55
Tobacco flags, felt, lot of 12, ca. 1906. $10
Sign, "Granger Tobacco", cardboard, WW-II soldier, 12 x 12 inches. $15
Pocket knife, bone-handled, "Y - B Cigars". $11
Tobacco tin, "Brandon Mixture / Richmond, VA", pocket-size. $20
Tobacco tin, "Honest Labor Cut Plug", very fine condition. $25
Lunch pail, "Dixie Queen Tobacco", litho. tin. $67.50
Sign, "Norseman Snuff", blue background, 8 x 16 inches. $22.50
Pocket tin, "Baghdad Tobacco". $50

Egg carrier and mailer, for six dozen eggs. Metal casing, label opening in top for name and address.

$25

Lar Hothem photo

Egg carrier and mailer, used for 15 dozen eggs, opening for mailing label at top.

$30

Lar Hothem photo

Container, tin, "Lucky Strike Cut Plug", hinged. $14

Tobacco tin, "J. C. Dills Best / Cube Cut Plug", 1910 tax
stamp. $8

Lunch pail, "Patterson's Seal Cut Plug". $30

Tobacco cannister, "Union Leader", 6 in. high. $18

Container, "Light Sweet Burley" tobacco. $55

Tobacco, tin, "Briggs Pipe Mixture", 1926 tax stamp. $9

Tobacco tin, 7 in. high, "Navy Snuff". $23

Cigar holder, amber glass, "Mercantile", lidded. $80

Sign, "Castle Hall / 5¢ Cigar", late 1800's, wood. $245

Tobacco tin, "Idle Hour Cut Plug", 1 x 2¾ x 4¾ inches. $28

Tobacco tin, "Beeswing Flaked Gold Leaf Cavendish",
pocket-size. $17

Container, tin, "Tuxedo Tobacco", 4½ in. high. $70

Cigar clippers, pocket-size, "Roitan". $22

Sign, "Just Say J. A. Cigars", litho tin, 2 x 20 in.,
ca. 1920. $30

Sign, cardboard, "Cyclone Twister 5¢ Cigar", 10 x 13 in.,
1929. $28

Tin, "Hiawatha Tobacco", 4-oz. size. $49

Sign, "Quail Cigars", cardboard, 3 x 12 in., quail shown,
1920's. $6

Sign, "Sunray 5¢ Cigar", 7 in. diameter, hanging, cardboard,
1930's. $5

Tobacco tin, "Hi-Plane Smooth-Cut", pict. monoplane,
5 x 6¼ inches. $50

Sign, "Y - B Cigars", cardboard, 20 x 30 inches. $25

Cigar box, brass hinges, "Golden Rule Cigars", five kinds
of wood. $60

Sign, "Harvester Cigars", tin, oval, 7 x 13 inches. $28

Cigar box, "Humo", tin, 9 in. wide. $9

Lunch box, "The Main Brace / Cut Plug", label.
1920's. $50

Container, tin, "Light Sweet Cuba Tobacco", 10½ in.
high. $135

Shoe-brush, "Bill Nye 5¢ Cigar", hardwood, 8½ in. long. $25

Lunch box, "Redicut Tobacco", fine lithograph. $90

Lunch pail, "Central Union Cut Plug", tin. $29

Sign, "Mayo's Plug Tobacco", canvas, poster, 24 x 40
inches. $85

Storage jar, glass, "Tuxedo Cigars". $40

Tobacco bag, "Just Suits / Cut Plug", 4½ x 5 inches. $5
Cigar box, wood, "Old Virginia Cheroots". $40
Ad., "Old Stock 5¢ Cigar", cardboard poster, 5 x 12 in.,
     1910's. $7
Tin, tobacco, "Salon", 1-lb. size. $24
Tobacco tin, "Pippins 5¢ Cigars", box for 25, 3 in. square. $45
Sign, tin, 'Piedmont / Virginia Tobacco", 11 x 11 inches. $38
Sign, "Velvet Tobacco", tin, framed, ca. 1910, 23 x 31
     inches. $350
Cigar box, Roosevelt, "Rough Rider", scarce. $85
Sign, "Phillip Morris", tin, 15 x 27 inches. $70
Pocket tin, "Epicure Tobacco", scarce. $60
Sign, "Target Tobacco", cloth, 1931, 30 x 56 inches. $65
Tin, pocket, "Twin Oaks Tobacco". $17
Tin, "Court Royal Cigars". $22.50
Box, "Boot Jack Chewing Tobacco", wood. $30
Tin, "Schinasi Bros Natural Egyptian Cigarettes". $28
Sign, tin, "Model Tobacco", picture of man, 4 x 12 inches. $30

Trade Cards

   Trade cards were printed cardboard avertisement that ranged
in size from business cards to 5 x 8 in. or larger. Many were about
the size of a postcard, and some could be used for that purpose.
Often, one side had an attractive picture, the reverse the message.
Most trade cards are not yet too expensive for the beginning collector,
and an endless range can be found. This is one area with much
growth potential due to the great number of cards in generally good
condition.

Card, "Buckingham Dye", colorful. $7
Card, "Domestic Sewing Machine", 5½ in. long. $6.25
Trade card, "Lion Coffee", good color. $5
Card, "Thomas Motor Bicycle / E. R. Thomas Motor Co. /
     Buffalo, N.Y." $12.50
Card, "E. O. Murphy / Harness Maker / Concord, N.H.". $4
Card, "Lion Coffee / Easter Greetings". $7
Card, "Shaker Extract of Roots / Cures Dyspepsia", 3¼ x
     5 inches. $15
Card, "Walter A. Wood Farm Machinery", Virginia
     Exposition. $8
Card, "Mayo's Diecut Tobacco", fine condition. $12.50

Trade-card, Ritter
Conserve Co., color-
ful. See reverse side
elsewhere.
Private collection

Advertising measuring stick, 2 feet long unfolded: "Plant Lime/
The Key To Fertility".

$7

Lar Hothem photo

Store items. L & R, advertising cards for Arm & Hammer Brand Soda and Saleratus, picturing different birds.

Each ... $1.25

Center, advertising dominoes, for "Volcanic Oil Linement / The Greatest Cure of Pain",
2 in. long.

Each ... $1.50

Hothem collection

Advertising rules. Top 6 in. "Churngold Oleomargarine".

$2.50

Middle, 6 in., "Lydic Meats" and cream-buyer.

$2.50

Bottom, 12 in., "LUXURY BREAD / No meal or lunch is quite complete / Unless there is Luxury Bread to eat".

$4.50

Private collection

Tin container. Slide-top, "Vantine's Incense / With its sweet breath vanishes all suggestion of the work-a-day world with its odors, its hustles, its cares".

$3

Lar Hothem collection

Gem Yeast trade-card, back, "If your Grocer does not keep them he can buy them of his Wholesale Grocer".

$4.25

Private collection

107

Card, "Columbus Buggy Company" (Ohio). $5

Card, "White Swan Soap", colorful, swan. $6

Card, "Heinz", showing product, fine. $5

Cards, "Singer", set of 40 (complete) dated 1892. $39

Card, "Shaker Family Pills / Cure Sick Headache". $18

Card, "Judson's Mountain Herb Pill", illus. of children
avoiding pain arrows. $6

Card, "Mrs. Pott's Cold-Handled Sad Iron / Portland, ME". $5

Card, "Rose Quesnel Smoking Tobacco / Rock City
Tobacco Co.". $4

Card, "Dr. Thomas Electric Oil / Cures Everything /
Earache In 2 Minutes". $8

Miscellaneous

Many listings did not fit conveniently into one of the previous
categories for one or another reason. They are presented here, in
the last section of Ch. VII. Many are one-of-a-kind, some very common, some rare, but all of interest to the store collector. Please keep
in mind the most important aspect of these collectibles, the condition. This will usually explain why an item may seem to be valued
high or low, in that the condition is either better than average, or,
below average.

Bank, advertising, "Nash Mustard", glass. $14

Fly swatter, "Swift", wire and screen, 1913. $15

Cracker Jack, "Book of Riddles". $20

Pin, shaped like pickle, "Heinz". $3.50

Poster, "Ferry Seed Co.", 32 in. high. $125

Prize, "Cracker Jack", pocket watch, tin. $35

Cake, "Snowflake Beeswax", round, 2 in. diameter. $2

Print, "Carter's Ink", 11 x 13 in., good color. $40

Calendar, 1930, "Delaval Separator", complete. $20

Bank, "Rival Dogfood", tin, shaped like can. $10

Blotter, "Kelloggs Corn Flakes", 3 x 6 in., 1918. $6

Booklet, "Chase & Sanborn", intact, "After Dinner
Tricks". $8

Tip tray, "President Suspenders", 4 in. diameter. $40

Market basket, bentwood handle, 23½ in. long. $45

Fan, advertising, "Burpee Seeds". $6

Bank, cat figure, metal, "Eveready". $11

Broadside, "Chippewa Salt — All Grades". $15

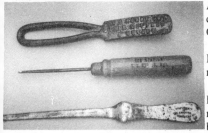

Advertising implements. Top, 7½ in. long, cast-iron fish-scaler, "C.D. Kenny Co./Teas, Coffees & Sugars".
$5

Middle, ice-pick, "Hebron Salt Co./Watermelons & Ice Cream Salt", 8 in. long.
$3.50

Bottom, letter-opener, 9¾ in. long, "Compliments of The Burrows Brothers Co.", blade bent.
$2.25

Private collection

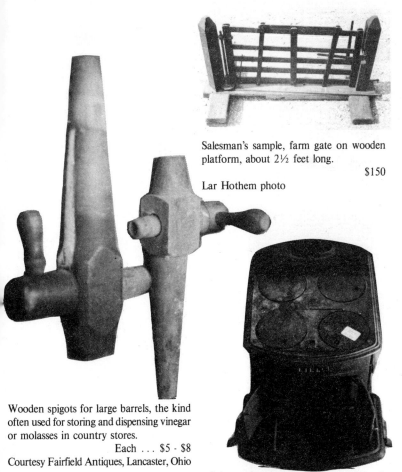

Salesman's sample, farm gate on wooden platform, about 2½ feet long.
$150

Lar Hothem photo

Wooden spigots for large barrels, the kind often used for storing and dispensing vinegar or molasses in country stores.
Each ... $5 - $8
Courtesy Fairfield Antiques, Lancaster, Ohio

Salesman's sample, wood- or coal-burning stove, by "Lilly".
$225

Lar Hothem photo

Whistle, "Cracker Jack", marked. $14

Jug, earthenware, "Hanson's Cider Mill". $26

Nut set, "Planters Peanuts", 5 pieces, metal. $18

Crate label, "Diving Girl Apples", 10 x 12 in., colorful,
1920's. $10

Tip tray, "S & H Green Stamps", woman shown, 1917. $45

Package and card, display, "Take Off Razor Blades". $9

Poster, tin-rimmed, "Yeast Foam", 10 x 14 in., 1920's. $40

Coin-operated machine, "Pulver", gumball, white. $340

Fan, "Bissels 'Cyco" Ballbearing Carpet Sweeper". $12

Display sign, tin, "Postum". $11

Button, advertising, "Davis Baking Powder". $6

Catalog, "Kelly Stove Co.", 1915. $18

Pen, "Stylographic", wood, over-sized, display-type. $25

Ruler, wood, "Crosley Radio'. $9

Booklet, "Parker Pen", fine condition, 1905. $23

Knife, "Picot Grape Salts", 3¼ in. long. $13

Book-mark, "Hood's Sarsaparilla", bright. $6

Tip tray, "Cottoline", Black woman and child in field,
4 in. diameter. $42.50

Tip tray, "New England Furniture & Carpet Co.", picture
of Priscilla Alden. $45

Store card with penknives, two dozen, all mint. $28

Eraser, for blackboard, "Belzer's General Store". $4

Catalog, "Brown & Sharpe Small Tools", 448 pages,
1926. $13

Booklet, childrens', "Chase & Sanborn Coffee and Tea
Importers". $9

Tip tray, "Welsbach Mantles", lamps around rim, eagle on
shield. $40

Matchbook, "Kenmore Vacuum Cleaners". $1

Pamphlet, "Crescent Bicycles", 1899, pictures. $20

Ration check, grocery store, WW-II. $1.50

Fly ribbon, "Big Chief", orig. cardboard box. $3

Print, framed, "Carter Ink Co. — Kittens". $27

Sign, window, "Minard's Linement', cardboard, two-fold. $25

Note pad, "Bromo Seltzer", 1920's. $7

Poster, WW-II, "Fisher Bodies / Keep America Free" series. $20

Billhook, celluloid over tin, "Black Cat Stove Polish", 2 in.
diameter, 1940's. $6

Doll, paper, "German Yeast Co.". $5

Poster, set of four, paper, "Kellogg's Breakfast Cereals".	$25
Blotter, celluloid baking, "Bakers Extracts".	$25
Box label, "Onetto Macaroni", 8 x 9 in., lady and factory, ca. 1900.	$6
Almanac, 1938, "Illinois Herb Co.".	$8
Ring, child's metal, "Post Toasties", 1940's.	$6
Bag, "Menora 5¢ Potato Chips", 3 x 7 in., 1920's.	$2
Billhook, "Johnson's Hats", 2 in. dia., celluloid over tin.	$7
Coloring book, "Mr. Peanut / American Heroes", 1935.	$18
Packs, "Burt's Seed Co. / N.Y.", 2½ x 3½ in., lot of 25, 1916.	$12
Ink blotter, "Chippewa Salt", good condition.	$4.50
Jar, glass, "Burma Shave", lidded.	$8
Tip tray, "Dowagiac / Grain Drills", grain on wood background.	$25
Pup figure, "Bucki / Carbon & Ribbons", cast-iron.	$23
Ruler, wood, 12-in., "Rival Dog Food".	$6
Booklet, "Borden's Baby Record", 1927.	$28
Letter opener, "Acme Grinders", metal, fine cond.	$8
Pan, "Watts Apple Pie", tin.	$18
Crate label, litho., "Kentucky Cardinal", 10 x 12 in., 1918.	$20
Puzzle, "Hood's Sasaparilla", original box.	$30
Ruler, wood, 6 in., "Nature's Remedy".	$3
Booklet, "Norton Abrasives / How To Sharpen", mint, 1935.	$5
Pickle fork, "Heinz 57", fine condition.	$14
Razor, "Gillette Eveready", tin container.	$7
Booklet, advertising, "Arm & Hammer Baking Soda".	$9
Calendar, all months, "Utica Club", 1939.	$70
Seed catalog, "Burpee's Annual — 1914".	$11
Letter opener, "Morris' Butter & Eggs", iron.	$8
Giveaway, frying pan, "Grand Union Tea Co.", 9-in. diameter.	$27
Pinback, "Peters Superior Cartridges".	$30
Booklet, "Western Ammunition", 1934.	$15
Pinback, "Buster Brown Shoes", colorful.	$23
Blotter, "Smith Bros. Cough Drops", w/Trade & Mark.	$7
Penknife, "Sunshine Biscuits", three-bladed, yellow.	$11
Bank, "Borgfeldt & Co. / NY", glass, Kewpie.	$85
Pinback, "Hood's Milk", good condition.	$6
Bottle, "Burnett's Standard Jamaica Ginger", 6½ in. high.	$9

Shoe-horn, metal, advertising for a Western general store: "Meyer & Locke Merc. Co.", 4 in. long.

$4

Private collection

Advertising salt and pepper shakers, l&r, "Ball" canning jar miniatures, unusual.

Pair ... $25

Center, "Atlas" canning jar bank, scarce, 3½ in. high, original.

$18

Lar Hothem photo

Store tin and humidor for Belfast cut plug cigars, "Smoke or Chew", 7 in. high.

$39

Private collection

Hold-to-light advertising card, front 3⅜ x 6 inches. When back-lighted, complete shoe ad. messages appears on the easel.

$5

Private collection

Manufacturer's trade-card, 3 x 5¼ in., black and white, by boot and shoe maker.

$2.25

Private collection

Mail Pouch outdoor thermometer, near mint condition, painted tin.

$65

Courtesy Robert A. Hodge, Candler, North Carolina

Fly ribbon, unused, "Holco Fly Catcher". $3
Token, brass, "Home Comfort Ranges". $11
Booklet, "Putnam Dye", good pages. $6
Blotter, "Kelly Tire", 4 x 9 in., 1920's. $3
Almanac, "Swamp Root", 1933. $9
Poster, "Remington,", bullet and shot loads / charges, 1923. $110
Tip tray, "White Rock Table Water", picture of Psyche. $50
Ink blotter, "Morton Salt', unused. $3.25
Peanut chopper, "Planter's", 1938. $12
Poster, "J.C. Penney's / Mickey Mouse", 19 x 26 in., 1935. $95
Catalog, "Savage Arms", early 1900's, colorful. $35
Almanac, "Kellogg's", intact, 1938. $13
Cigar band, "Buster Brown", paper, unusual, 1920's. $2
Blotter, "Arm & Hammer Soda", fine. $4
Cigar cutter, "Black & White 5¢ Cigars", pocket scissors
    type. $9
Paper-holder, leather-bound, "Edison Lamp Works". $8
Pocket knife, "Purina", all blades, checkerboard handle. $13
Jackknife, "E. H. Best & Co.". $12
Spice set, complete, "Aunt Jemima". $70
Tin, "Reed / Jamaica Ginger", ¼ pound size. $7
Good-luck token, "Worcestor Salt Company", 1920's. $9
Pamphlet, "Hocking Glass Co. / Lamps & Shades". $6
Button-hook, "Walk-Over Shoes", metal, folding. $8
Trade card, "Hersey Chocolate Co.", view of factory
    interior. $7

Chapter VIII

LONG DISTANCE LINES

Historic beginnings are always of interest, and the start of anything big and lasting has a positive fascination. In store days, all these lines were noteworthy, and some have lasted until today. In some instances, the name will be familiar, relating to available collectibles, while others may be unknown. (Ch. IX gives full product histories, with the business aspect to date.)

This chapter deals more with what once was, nostalgia from a certain perspective. These are highlights that perhaps the average collector is not aware of, but might like to know.

The oldest continuously run advertisement in U.S. commercial history is the Arm & Hammer Baking Soda ad. It appears on the inside-back cover of *The Old Farmer's Almanac,* and was first inserted in 1875. The *Almanac* is America's oldest continuously published periodical, established in the year 1792. In 1983, there were 3,845,400 copies distributed both here and abroad.

The "Brownies" characters once were featured on the advertisements of many coffee, cracker and soap makers. Brownies were fat little things with thin arms and legs, and huge eyes. They were the creation of artist and cartoonist Palmer Cox (b. 1840 - d. 1924) and became widely popular after their first appearance in a magazine poem in 1883. Cox had a huge old house (in Granby, Canada, Province of Quebec) which was called "Brownie Castle".

Graniteware was first manufactured in this country in the 1870's, and was designed for the then-new polished black kitchen stoves. Well-known early makers included LaLance & Grosjean of New York and Vollrath, of Wisconsin. This enamelware became necessary for any well-run kitchen by 1890, and replaced many tin, stoneware and cast-iron containers and utensils.

The Green River Works of New England was a highly respected name in solid, well-made knives of all kinds, and forks, spatulas and related utensils. Founded in 1834 by John Russell, the name was

Store ad. card, back, with line of products, twenty different foods.
Private collection

Store ad. card, front, blue flowers, cardboard, "Libby's Natural Flavor Food Products, 3½ inches.

$3.50

Private collection

The Plymouth Notch General Store, operated by John Coolridge, father of the U.S. President, when he married in 1868. In Calvin Coolidge's autobiography, he wrote, "The rent was $40 a year and by careful management profits averaged $100 a month". The building is ca. 1840, and was purchased by the State of Vermont in 1972.

Photo courtesy the State of Vermont Agency of Development and Community Affairs, Montpelier, Vermont

Store sign for Red Rose animal feeds, large size, enamel on steel, in poor condition.

$19

Private collection

Glass container, 4¾ in. high, "Black Flag / Not a Poison to Mankind and the Higher Animals When Used According to Instructions". Partial contents, full label.

$5

Private collection

Tin, no label, "Clabber Girl Baking Powder, 4⅜ in. high.

$3.50

Private collection

Bottle, for Singer Sewing Machine Oil, full label, printing on cap; 5¼ in. high.

$4

Private collection

changed after his retirement in 1868 to the John Russell Cutlery Company. Due to high quality, the factory's products were widely used, and they are heavily collected today.

In 1875, the Larkin Company of New York produced household products in great quantity. They offered valuable premiums like the Larkin desk and Haviland dinner sets. A 1915 cookbook, with Larkin ingredients, became a best-seller.

The Duryea brothers, in 1893, built the first successful American "horseless carriage", a word later shortened to "car". This motorcar was driven in Springfield, Massachusetts, and created much excitement. When country stores serviced the early cars, gasoline was carried out by hand, and put in the tank with the aid of a funnel.

The Waltham Watch Company, started by A. Dennison and E. Howard in 1850, was the first to mass-produce high-quality pocket watches. Over 30 million watches were made, but the growing popularity of the wristwatch helped close the business in 1950.

In 1898, National Biscuit Company's "Uneeda Biscuit" soda crackers were first put out in a sealed, moisture-proof package. It sold for five cents. A Golden Anniversary poster celebrated Nabisco's milestone and was put out in 1948.

In 1879, F.W. Woolworth opened his first store in Utica, New York. At the time, a fire-shovel sold for five cents. Due to a low volume of sales, he moved to a larger town nearby, and the rest is merchandising history.

A Mr. Cooper, in 1845, received an American patent for a gelatin dessert. The idea flowered around 1900, with "Jell-O", available in fruit and berry flavors.

The top-hatted Mr. Peanut, obviously a man of good taste, has been known from *SatEvePost* exposure since 1918. "The Planters Salted Peanuts" brand existed before then. Misters Obici and Peruzzi started in 1906 in Wilkes-Barre, Pennsylvania, and eventually had plants in San Francisco and Toronto, Canada. Many collectibles are associated with the name and figure.

———

About 1881, the Woolson Spice Company was founded in Toledo, Ohio. In addition to their famous "Lion" brand coffee, they — along with Arbuckle Coffee, well-received in the West — pioneered the use of fine premium cards. A.M. Woolson developed the idea of prepackaging coffee in tight, sanitary one-pound bags, and spices in smaller containers. The free trade cards, and holiday prints, are favorite items for today's collectors.

———

The "A & P" was one of the best of the first "chain" general food stores, the "Great Atlantic and Pacific Tea Company". By 1880, the company had nearly 100 stores in the eastern U.S. Their store colors were an eye-catching red and gold.

———

The dictionary states that "Moxie" was not only a soft drink, but the word entered the American language as courage, and the ability to face difficulty with spirit. It was begun by a Lieutenant Moxie, about 1884, and the soft drink was said to contain no alcohol or poisons, only good things. Moxie was heavily promoted, became very well known, and the drinks were dispensed from neighborhood wagons, a kind of mobile lemonade stands. There were many imitators, but Moxie survived into the 1940's. The product name is still used in New England.

———

The Watkins line of door-to-door products was started in Minnesota in 1868. The offerings competed strongly with the general store in spices and food concentrates, animal medicines and soaps. By 1930, nearly 150 different products were carried.

———

Franklin Miles, a physician, decided in 1884 to start a company in the home medication field. His initial capital was $1000, put up by two friends. Becoming Miles Laboratories, a health-care company, it was sold to Bayer AG, West Germany, in 1978. It now has more than one billion dollars in annual sales.

———

James Oliver, the famous plow-maker, was born in Scotland

in 1823, and emigrated to America at a young age. In 1855, he bought a quarter-interest in an iron foundry for $88.96 and began improving the plows they made. (Those of the day wore out both man and horses, and dirt had to be continually scraped from the moldboard with a wooden paddle.) Oliver spent 12 years perfecting a separate share and moldboard. According to The Roycrofters (Vol. 24, No. 2, 1909) the plow was "...nearly as bright as a diamond and about as hard, one that 'sang' at its work". Oliver's invention, the Chilled Plow, became the best-selling plow in the U.S. One of his favorite sayings was, "You benefit yourself only as you benefit humanity".

Purina-marked baby plate, with rabbit: "Find the bottom - - Um-m all gone". Blue glaze, 7 in. in diameter.

$32

Courtesy private collection

Chapter IX

HOUSEHOLD WORDS —
Famous Brand Names

There are many names that were around in Country Store days that are still here, having weathered time, competition, even the stress of success. The products were purchased "off the shelf" for many years, and perhaps our children's children will enjoy them. All began well before 1950, some more than a hundred years ago with strong roots in native soil. Most brands will have a familiar ring of a tried-and-true product, almost a family friend.

But more than business-writing (this chapter), and the public-relations (the source), the central theme is purely American. Each represents a good product (this country's or from abroad), long, hard work, and a little bit of luck. The origins are fascinating, with small beginnings long ago. Then came development, and changes to address the needs of the times, always meeting requirements at a fair price.

Some products were total innovations, while others improved on similar items. All, however, were viewed by buyers as well worth the money. Consumers have always been a wary bunch, balancing dollars against worth. The brand-name products listed here all have proven acceptance, and inspiration and practicality met happily in the marketplace.

There's a lesson for us all here: The average tends to hang around for awhile, then disappear — or as they used to say, "fall by the wayside". The best lasts, as you will see. Here, then, are some famous household words, very much store-related.

BURPEE SEEDS

The W. Atlee Burpee Company started business in 1876. A few years later, the Company began making items (listed in the Burpee Seed Catalog) available to stores and selling bulk seeds to dealers. A Company slogan since the 1890's has been, "Burpee Seeds Grow"; this is being shifted now to "Burpee Gardens Grow" to better reflect the whole field of gardening.

The seed color packet business for Burpee started in the mid-1930's, probably about 1936. Today, some general merchandise is handled in stores, such as "Seeds 'n Starts", set up in special displays, as well as the standard Burpee packet racks. The focus remains on top-notch seed varieties and products for the home gardener. Part of the company logo is, "The Gardening People".

CAMPBELL SOUPS

When the Frenchman N. Appert discovered a successful food-canning method in 1809, he started a new industry. Many later canners made use of the process, involving sealed containers and heat sterilization. Among them were Abram Anderson, an ice-box maker, and Joseph Campbell, a fruit merchant. Their partnership was formed in 1869, in Camden, New Jersey, and their preserved foods quickly became popular.

In 1891, the Company became the Jos. Campbell Preserve Co., and the concept of Canned Condensed Soup was developed in 1897.

Example of early Campbell's Soup ad., which appeared in the June 1916, *National Geographic*.

The distinctive red-and-white label was introduced in 1898, suggested by the football uniforms of Cornell College. And the gold medallion (for excellence) was awarded at the 1900 Paris Exposition.

The trademark Campbell Kids, a rosy-cheeked boy and girl, were created by Grace Gebbie, a Philadelphia artist, in 1904. The first national magazine ad. appeared in *Good Housekeeping* in 1905, which noted, "21 Kinds of Campbell's Soups / 16 million cans sold in 1904". National Distribution was achieved in 1911, with entry into the California market. In 1922, the name was changed to Campbell Soup Company, and radio advertising was begun in 1931.

The company started to manufacture their own cans in 1936; though they produce for their own needs only, they are the third largest food can maker in the world. In 1942, Campbell sales went over the $100 million mark.

Today, Campbell makes over 750 high-quality convenience foods, and brand names like "V-8", Pepperidge Farm, Franco-American and Vlasic are easily recognized. The Company has 78 plant locations in the U.S. and in 12 foreign countries, making Campbell one of the world's great food processors.

COLEMAN LAMPS And LANTERNS

In the late 1890's, a Kansas school-teacher and part-time salesman named William C. Coleman discovered an unusual lamp in the window of an Alabama drugstore. It burned pressurized gasoline, vaporizing and igniting it in a flame-proof fabric mantle, itself invented in 1885. It was called the Efficient lamp, made by the Edward Miller Co. of Meriden, Connecticut. In a day of coal-oil lamps and the early carbon filament electric bulbs (invented 1879), the lamp gave a steady, bright, low-cost light.

Coleman purchased a number of the lamps from the Tennessee firm of Irby-Gilliland and went West to sell, but found little market. Realizing he must sell lighting, not just promises, Coleman started the Hydro-Carbon Light Co. in 1900. Renting his lamps for a dollar per week, before long his stopping-place (Kingfisher, Oklahoma) was a bright spot on the prairie.

Moving to Wichita, Kansas, in 1901, Coleman purchased all rights to the Efficient in 1902, improving what he now called the Coleman Arc Lamp. In 1905, Coleman began to make his own lamps. Further contact with storekeepers convinced him that "System Lighting" was possible. Successful, this was a central gasoline device connected to numerous fixtures, much like central electricity today.

Coleman also worked on portable lamps or lanterns, and in 1909 received a patent on his "Model R" (for reading), later improved into the "Air-O-Lite". In 1914, the first Coleman lanterns appeared, adapted for outdoor use; these were the "Arc Lanterns". A patented 1916 innovation was match-lighting, a simpler process than heating the generator before operation.

Many other kinds of lighting, heating, cooking and ironing products were made. A 1916-1930 slogan was, "The Sunshine of the Night".

CREAM OF WHEAT

The mill town of Grand Forks, North Dakota, was suffering the effects of the Panic of 1893. At the Diamond Milling Company, flour prices were down and demand was reduced. Processing fewer than a thousand bushels a day, the flour sold for only $2 a hundred pounds.

A mill employee, Tom Amidon, had been taking home some "middlings" — unused wheat hearts — for a homemade hot breakfast porridge. He liked the result so much he convinced the mill owners to include ten cases in a New York City flour shipment. On the spur of the moment, bystanders named the product "Cream Of Wheat", hand-lettering it on the shipping containers.

Three hours after the shipment reached its destination, back came a telegram. It read: "Forget the flour. Send us a car of Cream Of Wheat". Within a year the market had increased to the extent that a Cream Of Wheat Corporation was set up in Minneapolis and national advertising was begun.

One of the famous artworks of the time depicted a mounted mail rider delivering mail to a mailbox made from a Cream Of Wheat packing box. The logo, "Where the mail goes Cream Of Wheat goes", was popular at the time. Advertisements ran mainly in magazines and used four-color printing, a novelty then.

Cream Of Wheat ads. had some famous illustrators, among them James Montgomery Flagg, designer of the Wartime Uncle Sam recruiting posters. Today, Cream Of Wheat is part of the brand family of NABISCO BRANDS.

DOLE PINEAPPLE

James Drummond Dole arrived in Hawaii in 1899, a time when pineapples were commercially grown on a small scale, largely ornamental plants for gardens. A Harvard graduate and native of Boston, Dole took an interest in the spectacular, good-tasting fruit. In 1901, he planted 12 acres in central Oahu, 20 miles from Honolulu, and built a small cannery. His production, in 1903, was only 1873 cases.

Sugar was then the region's major crop, and the attitude toward pineapple was summed up by a Honolulu newspaper of the time. "If pineapple paid, the vacant lands near town would be covered with them". Dole went ahead anyway. So novel was the pineapple that Dole included instructions in his ads.: "You eat it with a spoon, like a peach".

Gradually, Americans came to accept pineapples, and Dole was in business. A Company "first" was the machine developed by Henry Ginaca, beginning in 1911, which removed the pineapple's outer shell and core at the rate of 30 units per minute. This permitted mass processing, and Dole became a major canner.

Dole is the world's leading producer of fresh and canned pineapple, and the Company cannery in Honolulu is the largest in the world. Some 175 million pineapples are processed each year. This production goes into slices, chunks and crushed pineapple, as well as juice. The latter is single-strength for the consumer market, plus juice and concentrates for food services and industrials.

Dole is now (acquired, 1961) wholly owned by Castle & Cooke, Inc., a firm that has been in Hawaii since 1851. The Dole brand name is applied to pineapples, bananas, and fresh mushrooms.

DURKEE FAMOUS SAUCE

Eugene R. Durkee, in 1857, created a food product and marketed it door-to-door from his home in Brooklyn, New York. Originally named "Durkee's Dressing", the condiment is now called "Famous Sauce". It has been used as a flavoring for meats, seafood, salads, vegetables and many other dishes, and President Lincoln is thought to have asked that it be served in the White House.

Antique Durkee bottles contained either this dressing or Challenge Sauce (Worcestershire) and are imprinted with the name

E. R. Durkee & Co. Company literature states that "... the embossed 'Gauntlet Brand' trademark is visible on many bottles. (The) medieval armored glove stood for protected flavor and strength... Frequently the year 1873 is embossed on the bottle, which represents the patent date of the container. Cylindrical bottles with a short neck contained Salad Dressing, and the slender bottle with a long neck contained Challenge Sauce."

Mr. Durkee's original business was the preparation and sale of extracts, spices and related products, starting in 1850. He became so respected for integrity that the government requested that he help write specifications for the spice industry in the 1906 Pure Food Laws.

Glidden acquired Durkee in 1929, and, along with other acquisitions, these were brought under the name Durkee Famous Foods. The three main subdivisions today are industrial foods, food service, and consumer foods. Now owned by SCM Corporation, Durkee is the country's largest importer of Spanish green olives, the second largest marketer of coconut, and the second largest processor and marketer of spices, herbs and seasonings.

FEDERAL CARTRIDGES

The Federal Cartridge and Machinery Company began at Anoka, Minnesota, in 1916, but achieved little success until 1922. Then, Charles L. Horn became managing partner of a new company, the Federal Cartridge Corporation. By late 1922, the Company was offering "Hi-Power" shotgun shells, and .22 rimfire rounds were added in 1924.

The Company did considerable work for the U.S. government during WW-II, Korea, and Vietnam. Cartridges produced for the military effort ranged from .50 caliber machine-gun rounds to 5.56 mm for rifles. The cartridge headstamp has been "TW". This ammunition was made in nearby New Brighton, where a peak WW-II production figure of ten million rounds per day was reached.

Finalized in 1963, the Federal line of ammunition included its own brand of pistol and rifle centerfire rounds. Today, a very wide range of sporting ammunition is manufactured. The Company offers shotshells from 10-gauge to .410, rifled slugs, trap-loads, rifle ammunition from .222 to .45-70 calibers, and pistol and revolver rounds from .22 to .45. The .22 alone has a dozen varieties.

A Company motto has been, "Ammo You Can Count On".

GULDEN'S MUSTARD

Gulden's was established in 1862 by Charles Gulden, prior to his serving in the Civil War. The Company location was Elizabeth Street in downtown New York City. The business began with limited capital, but quickly prospered and grew.

According to the Company, ". . . Distribution in those early days was confined to the distance one could drive and work a team and return at night within the then usual 12-14 hour day. However, the exceptional quality of the Gulden product was quick to gain acceptance and its fame spread by word of mouth from the limits of horse-drawn distribution to areas beyond."

Gulden's Mustard won various Certificates and Gold Medals between 1869 and 1926; in 1883 the Company moved to larger quarters at 46-58 Elizabeth Street. At that time, some 30 varietes of mustard were being produced, plus other condiments and foods such as capers and olives. Eventually, the production concentrated only on mustard.

In 1962, Charles Gulden, Sr., a grandson of the founder, sold the Company to American Home Foods, of New York City. The Gulden Kitchens are at Milton, Pennsylvania. The ultra-modern facilities produce the original Brown Mustard, Yellow Mustard (added in 1947) and Hot Diablo Mustard (1960).

The recipes are secret blends of pure mustard seeds, and rare spices and vinegars. A Company motto is: "The Standard of Quality since 1862".

HILLS BROS. COFFEE

The year was 1873, California was growing, and Mr. Austin Hills brought his family to San Francisco from New England. Mr. Hills, a ship-builder, constructed ferry-boats for The Bay, but his sons, Austin H. and Reuben W., took a different tack. In the spring of 1878, they started a retail store, the "Arabian Coffee and Spice Mills".

Quoting from Company literature, it ". . . grew quickly, selling coffee, tea, spices, extracts, butter and eggs direct to consumers. By 1886, the horse-and-buggy door-to-door deliveries were discontinued and were replaced by exclusive marketing to grocery outlets". Reuben pioneered "cup-testing", evaluating coffee beans not on how they looked, but on aroma and taste.

The Company plant was destroyed in the 1906 earthquake; a

Store window display of Hills Bros. Coffee, cans and advertising signs.
Photo courtesy Hills Bros. Coffee, Inc., San Francisco, California

move was made to temporary quarters for several years, and a new plant was built in 1908. Hills Bros.' success was based on vacuum-packing (which they originated in 1900). This allowed ground coffee to remain fresh indefinitely. This also meant expanded distribution and earned a national reputation for quality. In 1926 a modern facility was completed in San Francisco, where Hills Bros. headquarters remain today.

New bean-roasting operations were started in Edgewater, New Jersey, in 1941 to meet expanded demand for Hills Bros. coffee. Products since that time include Instant coffee, Mocha beverages, High-Yield coffee which produces more cups per pound, and Decaffeinated coffee.

HOPPE'S NO. 9 SOLVENT

In the early part of the 20th Century, smokeless powder began to replace blackpowder in cartridges and shotshells. Both were extremely corrosive materials, and cleaning a firearm was a long, hard task. One man, Frank August Hoppe, born in 1879, found a better way. Trained and experienced as a chemist, and with interests in sports and soldiering, Mr. Hoppe began experimenting.

According to Company literature, "He began to think in terms of a chemical or combination of chemicals to simplify the dirty job of cleaning rifle bores. His aim was to develop a product that would remove all primer, powder, lead and metal fouling from the rifle bore while at the same time protecting it from rust."

In 1903, the Frank A. Hoppe Company was founded, and he began to produce the combination of nine chemicals known as "Hoppe's Nitro Powder Solvent No. 9". Word had earlier spread about the solvent's unique properties, and the Company's success was assured. Mr. Hoppe died in 1921, and the business was left to his wife Mary and a 15-year-old son, Frank C. Mrs. Hoppe's brother, Charles A. Rasmussen, helped operate the Company, and in 1928 Frank C. Hoppe became president.

In 1940, Frank C. donated the Frank A. Hoppe Memorial Trophy, awarded annually at NRA meetings. A wide range of products relating to the care of firearms was developed. Eventually, in 1968, the Company was acquired by Penguin Industries, Inc., and the Corporation added new products to the long-established Hoppe line.

A 1921 ad. refers to No. 9 Solvent as "The greatest boon to the modern rifleman", a position it holds to this day. It does appear to be the perfect solution.

KIWI POLISH

John Ramsay and his family migrated from Scotland to Melbourne, Australia in 1878. By 1906 a son, William, had developed an "unusually fine" boot polish, which he called "Kiwi". This was in tribute to his wife, a native of New Zealand, home of the flightless, long-beaked Kiwi bird.

During a visit to New Zealand in 1900, William had noticed the fine, glossy plumage of the bird, and decided its likeness enhanced the cover of the round tin in which the polish was packed. Also, the name was short, attractive, and easy to remember.

WW-I vastly increased sales because soldiers' boots needed to be kept in top shape. And, the Australian Light Horse troops with leather accoutrements became "walking advertisements" for Kiwi Polish. By 1917 the British and American armies were placing huge orders for the polish, and other Allied armies followed suit.

During WW-II, American troops became familiar with the famous "parade shine" imparted by Kiwi, a shine that lasted and had "reserve" powers that could be brought back by a quick buffing. Also, the Company's product nourished the leather, making it pliant, covering scuffs, keeping it new-looking.

By 1940, there were four Kiwi factories in Australia, New Zealand, France and England. In 1948, another was opened in Philadelphia, to keep up with domestic demand. Kiwi Polish has become the fastest-growing shoe polish in America.

Today Kiwi markets a wide range of footwear care products including shoe laces, shoe brushes, insoles, etc. as well as liquid, creme and the paste polishes.

LIPTON TEA

On his 21st birthday, Thomas Johnstone Lipton — having already been to America where he earned $500 — opened a second family food store in Glasgow. The year was 1871, and before long Lipton owned 20 stores across Scotland, eventually hundreds. By 1890, a millionaire, he sailed for Australia and Ceylon. Buying plantations cheaply in Ceylon, Lipton was suddenly in the tea business.

Before his arrival, Ceylon tea was harvested in the mountains and slowly packed down meandering trails to factories in the valleys. Lipton used a system of aerial wires, and bags of tea leaves slid right to the factory where they were machine-processed. Some London friends devised a special blend of teas, and all proclaimed the result superior. An early slogan was, "Direct from the Tea Gardens to the Tea Pot", and, "Millions drink it Daily".

Lipton's stores carried his tea and the public clamored for it. Reports the Company, "...A Lipton branch which didn't sell at least a ton of tea every week was considered at headquarters to be slipping". An innovation was packaging tea in 1, ½ and ¼ pound "packets" so the buyer knew price, weight and quality. This helped make England a tea-drinking nation. For his trade contributions and charity gifts, Lipton was knighted by Queen Victoria in 1898.

He sold much tea in the U.S. and Canada, marketing tea bags to restaurants, hotels and homes. By 1927, the bag manufacturing process was automatic, all tea selected by expert tasters and master blenders.

Thomas L. Lipton, Inc., operating today from Englewood Cliffs, New Jersey, has also diversified into other fields. These are trademark names like Wish-Bone salad dressings, Good Humor ice cream, Knox gelatine, and Pennsylvania Dutch noodles. Sir Thomas would have been pleased.

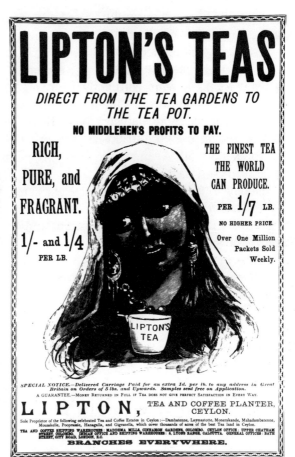

The first Lipton Tea ad., 1892. Satisfaction was guaranteed, or "...Money returned in full...".

Photo courtesy Thomas J. Lipton, Inc., Englewood Cliffs, NJ

LUDEN'S COUGH DROPS

More than 100 years ago, in 1881, a William H. Luden made a batch of candy in his mother's tiny kitchen, and peddled it on the streets of his hometown, Reading, Pennsylvania. Known as "moshie", the sweet was made with brown sugar and corn syrup. Response was tremendous, so the young man hired an assistant and placed his candies directly with local storekeepers. His business flourished.

Candy-flavored cough remedies were widely available, but Luden and a Reading pharmacist worked on a different idea. They added menthol to their drop, which actually soothed dry, scratchy throats and came up with a market innovation. Luden knew his product was better than others on the market, all of which were red. Against advice, he colored the new Luden's Cough Drop amber, and, reports Company literature, "...the rest is history".

Expanding his production facilities twice in 1887, Luden moved his factory to its present location in Reading in 1910. He ran the Company for many years, constantly improving quality, always looking for innovations. Some of the mixing machines Luden designed are still used in the candy industry today. Before, mixing was a backbreaking job for even the strongest men. In 1936, Luden came out with the famous 5th Avenue candy bar, processing all the materials in the Company factory.

Today, Luden's facilities cover eight acres, with a thousand employees during peak production months. The Company is one of the top ten U.S. candy manufacturers, and one of the top three cough drop makers. Luden's products are sold in 72 countries, and a 100th Anniversary celebration was held in 1981. The writer fondly remembers Luden's Cough Drops as one candy that could be enjoyed in the schoolroom, accompanied by appropriate coughs.

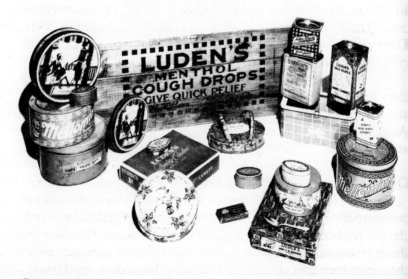

Early packaging in tin containers, for Luden's Cough Drops, Silk Gloss Candies, Iceland Mints and Mellomints.

Photo courtesy Luden's, Incorporated, Reading, Pennsylvania

MARLIN FIREARMS

John M. Marlin, born in Connecticut in 1836, learned the trade of tool and die making. He worked at the Colt factory in Hartford during the Civil War, and in 1870, started his own business in New Haven. He formed The Marlin Fire-Arms Company in 1880. His original product line included derrringers, pistols and revolvers, made until 1899.

The Company's emphasis has always been quality, and their shoulder arms are without equal. Their Model 39 (a .22 rifle, lever-action, introduced in 1891) is the oldest rifle design still being manufactured in the world. The Marlin Model 336 (a high-power repeater, introduced as the Model 1893) is the second oldest. Over five million firearms of both models have been sold.

Marlin also produced the single-shot, long-range Ballard target/hunting rifle from 1875 until about 1890, with calibers from .22 to .50. According to Company literature, the action ". . .closed like a well-oiled safe". Another success was the most powerful repeating rifle of its day, popular in the West. This was the Model 1881, firing the military .45/70 round.

Other products were manufactured; early catalogs, in addition to firearms, also list a shoehorn/buttonhook, decoy anchors and hand-cuffs. The Company became the Marlin Rockwell Company in 1916. During WW-I infantry and aircraft machine-guns and automatic rifles were produced.

In 1923 it was reorganized as the Marlin Firearms Corporation and again in 1926, the Company changed ownership, and is still owned by the Kenna family. Marlin firearms users included Annie Oakley known as "Little Miss Sure Shot", and silent-screen star, Tom Mix.

OCEAN SPRAY CRANBERRIES

Cranberries — there are over 100 varieties — have never been commercially grown other than in North America. Indians first used the tart red berries as an ingredient in dried pemmican. The Pilgrims thought the pink blossoms resembled the heads of cranes and called them crane-berries, eventually shortened to the modern word. Berry vines take 3 to 5 years until harvest, but can produce indefinitely; some cranberry bogs have been worked for over 100 years.

The Ocean Spray story begins with Marcus L. Urann, president of the Cape Cod Cranberry Company. He was dismayed by

Marlin firearms: Top, the Model 1881 (Serial no. 1); middle, Model 1888; bottom, Model 1889.

Photo courtesy The Marlin Firearms Company, North Haven, Connecticut

Marlin firearms: Shotguns (top) the Model 43 trap; bottom, the Model 43, made 1920-1930.

Photo courtesy The Marlin Firearms Company, North Haven, Connecticut

excess harvests that spoiled, and decided processing was the answer. He developed a cranberry sauce "like homemade", helped make the first batch, designed the label, and went out and sold it. Highly successful, he earned the nickname "Cranberry King".

Mr. Urann's canning operation was the Ocean Spray Preserving Company. The Ocean Spray brand name came from the salt mists that drifted over the cranberry bogs. The label was "Ocean Spray Cape Cod Cranberry Sauce". The first can was packed in Hanson, Massachusetts, in 1912, and a second plant was located in Onset.

Ocean Spray, a grower's cooperative, joined with two others in 1930 to maintain quality and extend the industry. The Massachusetts and New Jersey growers/owners had four canning facilities.

Homemakers welcomed the product, and Ocean Spray expanded into Wisconsin, Oregon and Washington. During WW-II, cranberries were dehydrated for the Armed Services. The first million-barrel crop was harvested in 1953, with 58% going to Ocean Spray. Today, there are processing plants in four states, all designed to meet present and anticipated production needs.

OREO COOKIES

In 1912, the National Biscuit Company launched three varieties of biscuit products, these all being ". . . highest class biscuit packed in a new style". These were, the Mother Goose with impressions from the various childrens' stories, and the sweet, hard Veronese with a fine design. The third offering, the Oreo, is described in Company literature as, ". . . two beautifully embossed, chocolate-flavored wafers with a rich cream filling."

The first two products, created with great expectations, are no longer around. But the Oreo caught on quickly, to become the best-selling cookie in the world. To date, over 100 *billion* have been sold. Stacked, this number would reach twice to the moon, and back. Oreo size has varied over the years, and today's version is mid-size between the largest and smallest.

The name also has changed. It was first the Oreo Biscuit, in 1921 the Oreo Sandwich, in 1948 the Oreo Creme Sandwich, and in 1974, the Oreo Chocolate Sandwich Cookies. Strangely, the origin of the name itself is uncertain. It may be Greek for "mountain", after an early experimental shape. Or, it may be French for "gold", the color of the original label and product name, both set on a pale green background.

Certainly one attractive feature of the Orea was the medallion size and appearance, seemingly very expensive but at a reasonable price. And, the chocolate-and-cream flavors, always American favorites, combined nicely together.

Oreo is another member of the NABISCO BRANDS family; the Biscuit Division alone has some 108 different products.

PILLSBURY FLOUR

When John Sargent Pillsbury arrived in St. Anthony Falls (later to be known as Minneapolis) it was the year 1855. He started a general and hardware store, destroyed by fire two years later. By 1869, he had rebuilt the hardware business and his political status, which led three times to the governorship. He sent back East for a bright nephew, Charles A. Pillsbury, who arrived with both ambition and bride that same year.

Charles, with two other men, bought into an old flour mill, one capable of 200 barrels a day. He set out to increase flour quality by making better milling equipment. He and his millers and machinists improved the device that cleaned and graded ground wheat, the middlings purifier. This brought about "high grinding". The mill turned a profit that year, and the Pillsbury name was launched.

In 1872, the "Pillsbury's Best" brand was registered. He began to plan the largest flour mill in the world, really two under one roof. Housing the very latest in equipment, including steel rollers rather than grindstones, the Pillsbury mill eventually covered 115 by 175 feet. Built of massive sandstone blocks, it soared 187 feet, from basement wheat bin to the roof peak. The separate units were known as "East A" and "West A".

Operations began in 1881, and 4000 barrels of flour a day was ground. Fires destroyed other Pillsbury mills, but the new mill was able to increase production. In 1882, 90 "plansifter" devices replaced some 1870 other conveyors, reels and gears, while increasing production and lowering power requirements. Pillsbury's "Ninth Wonder of the World" ground a record 16,113 barrels in one day in 1905.

Production would have been pointless without the great demand for a fine flour. This Charles Pillsbury offered — and provided.

RED STAR YEAST

In the late 1880's, Milwaukee's National Distilling Company's yeast sideline had different product names. The best known was Red Star®, the yeast handcut and foil-wrapped at tables. First marketed by horse-drawn delivery van, the by-product was used for commercial and home baking, and later, as a health aid as well.

A modern distribution system for the times, early 1900's, Red Star® Yeast became famous throughout the country.

Photo courtesy Universal Foods Corporation, Milwaukee, Wisconsin

Well-proven, Red Star® achieved rapid growth. In 1893 there were eight upper Midwestern distribution centers; in 1917, thirty-three; a few years after 1921, eighty. Prohibition (1919-1933) cut into liquor sales, but the yeast branch thrived, aided by a 1918 German aeration yeast-making process, with later Company improvements.

Red Star® did very well as a food supplement, and 1930's delivery trucks announced: "New large cake, 2 for 5¢ / Here's Health, 2 Cakes Daily". Premiums for Red Star® purchases included silver-plated tableware of 21 kinds, plus damask towels and linen tablecloths. An innovation was an inert nitrogen atmosphere inside the foil package to protect the live yeast.

By WW-II, research into yeast properties developed active dry yeast for military baking, and some five million pounds were produced for overseas use alone. The Post-War popularity of homemade hot rolls further increased Red Star® use. In 1951, a yeast plant was constructed at Belle Chasse, Louisiana, and in 1955, Consumer's Yeast Corporation of San Francisco was purchased. This made the Company a national yeast supplier.

Seeking expansion, Red Star® went public in 1961, and the Company changed its name to Universal Foods Corporation. Now, with Red Star® manufacturing facilities in four locations throughout the U.S., the Company produces the world's most diversified line of yeast products. A century old in 1982, Corporate product-lines include beverage, cheese, fermentation (over 67 yeast varieties), import, and specialty items.

SCHRADE KNIVES

Schrade Cutlery Company was founded in 1904 by the Shrade brothers. From small early beginnings, the Company expanded to the point where nearly 600 models were offered in the 1920's and '30's. The Company has always stressed high quality, and their trademark has been, "Everlastingly Sharp".

There has always been fine attention to basic details. As stated in their 1926 catalog: "Next in importance to selecting the right steels for blades and springs is the designing and heat treatment of the same."

The Company survived the Depression and produced a number of fighting knives for personnel of the Armed Services in WW-II. In the late 1940's, Albert and Henry Baer bought the Company from Louis Schrade, one of the original founders. It then became the Schrade Walden Cutlery Corp., part of the Imperial Knife Associated Companies, Inc.

Later, the original plant at Walden, New York (another, estab. 1917, was at Middletown) was moved to Ellenville, New York, where Schrade remains today. Nearly 100 styles are made, including the popular "Old Timer" and "Uncle Henry" knives.

SHEAFFER PENS

The year was 1907, and a successful Iowa jeweler named Walter A. Sheaffer (born, 1867) read a newspaper ad. for a pen. The filling device included an unsightly hump on the barrel to deflate an ink sac, this in a day when most pens were filled with an eyedropper. Sheaffer found an answer to such problems.

He eliminated both the eyedropper and the filling hump by devising a simple level and pressure bar to deflate the sac, which drew up ink by suction. The bar itself was flush with the barrel, and now an attractive pen part. The improvements were not only innovative; they worked.

A patent was issued in 1908, another in 1912 which covered a better lever and pressure bar. In 1912 Sheaffer set up a small manufacturing shop in the back of his jewelry store, engaged salesmen, and started out. In six months, the pens were selling faster than his half a dozen workers could make them, and in 1913, he moved the operation into larger quarters in Fort Madison. About two years later, the Company moved again, and in 1917 Sheaffer expanded with the purchase of a former plow factory.

Sales dropped during the Great Depression, but the Company weathered a loss in 1933. Precision instruments were made for the WW-II effort, and an Army-Navy "E" Award was received in 1944. In 1952, an ultra-modern office and factory was completed in Fort Madison, in a lovely setting overlooking the Mississippi River. In 1953, a third plant was built in that home community.

The Company has always produced writing instruments of high quality. Sheaffer Pens is now Sheaffer Eaton Division of Textron Inc. As a personal endorsement, the first draft of this book was written using four Sheaffer fine-point pens.

SMUCKER'S PRESERVES

In 1897 Jerome M. Smucker began a custom apple cider mill in the Central Ohio town of Orrville, in the rich agricultural soils of Wayne County. It went well, and later apples were cooked with cider to make a tasty apple butter. The old-fashioned recipe came from David Smucker, Jerome's grandfather, from Pennsylvania Dutch country.

J.M. Smucker's apple butter business prospered, and a full line of preserves (made from whole fruit or pieces of fruit) and jellies (made from strained pure fruit juice) was added in the 1920's. In 1935, the Company expanded into the state of Washington, the first of Smucker's extensive Northwestern U.S. operations. National distribution began in 1942, with a shipment of preserves and jellies from Orrville to Los Angeles.

The Company purchased Mary Ellen, Inc., a West Coast producer of jams and jellies, in 1963 and a Pennsylvania peanut butter processing plant was acquired in 1965. In 1979, the Company bought the Dickinson Family, Inc., makers of gourmet preserves and jellies. Corporate offices today remain in Orrville, with fresh fruit processing plants in Watsonville and Oxnard, California, Grandview, Washington, and Woodburn, Oregon. Manufacturing plants are located in Orrville, Memphis, Tennessee and Salinas, California.

Today, the J.M. Smucker Company is the country's number one producer of preserves, jams and jellies, its main products being these plus fruit butters, marmalades, ice cream toppings and fruit syrups. The Company services eight major markets: Grocery, Foodservice, Industrial, General Merchandise, Specialty Foods, Gifts and Incentives, Government and Export. Their advertising slogan is, "With a name like Smucker's, it has to be good".

VICTOR MOUSETRAP

Build a better mousetrap . . . and one man indeed did. John Mast, in the late 1800's, worked to perfect a simple, inexpensive "snap-shot" trap. He added a larger-size rat-trap, and the two proved so successful that in 1902 he moved to another town in the state, Lititz, Pennsylvania, and erected a new trap-making building.

In 1907, Mast's company was acquired by the Oneida Community, a business/religious group that had pioneered in the field with their Newhouse brand. In 1924, three Community executives (including C.M. Woolworth, Woodstream's Chairman of the Board until 1977) purchased the firm and renamed it the Animal Trap Company of America. In 1925, Oneida's wildlife trap business was acquired and also moved to Lititz.

Now a part of Woodstream Corporation, the Victor-brand mouse- and rat-trap products are still favorites, still as effective now as nearly 90 years ago. Woodstream itself is a broad-based manufacturing Company that specializes in many kinds of sturdy and innovative sporting goods, for hunting, fishing and boating. Their extensive work for the government in WW-II resulted in several articles, entitled "From Mouse Traps To Bullets".

According to the Company, "Demand for . . . wildlife traps is also still growing due to worldwide demand for raw furs, the necessity of farmers, ranchers and stockmen to protect their crops and livestock from predatory animals, and the increasing need for these products in the maintenance of a reasonable balance of wildlife in our environment."

WRIGHT'S SILVER CREAM

In 1872, John A. Wright noticed a cow stuck in a bog near Keene, New Hampshire. After helping extricate the animal, he saw that the mud was very unusual, and took samples to be analyzed. It was very pure diatomaceous or "float-stone", produced by long-ago marine organisms. The material was well-suited as a polishing agent. Mr. Wright bought the bog, drained it, and erected a building in 1873.

The original product name was "Red Star Cleaning Powder", also marketed as "Golden Seal Metal Polish". Nearby dealers and hotel owners quickly ordered supplies, and a wheelbarrow took shipments to the railroad station. At first the powder was packaged in small cardboard boxes or round wooden containers. Mr. Wright saw that a self-contained paste form might be better than loose powder. This was done, and the present name, "Silver Creme", was registered in 1887.

Red Star Cleaning Powder was made for a number of years afterward, printed paper boxes giving way to tin. Polishing powder was discontinued in 1934, and had been used for metals, tile, glass and teeth. At the turn of the century, Silver Cream was being packaged in glass containers, with a half-pint jar selling for 25¢. A sample-size miniature jar was introduced in 1909.

A new factory was built in 1941, and the Company made their own labels, itself a successful printing business. Beginning in 1896, Wright's was the first silver cream to be nationally advertized. Today, the product bases a highly successful family-run business. The Cream's familiar, pleasant smell? It's sassafras.

Chapter X

TIPS FOR THE STORE SHOPPER

One can find country store related goods almost anywhere. These range from the omni-present small tins to larger fixtures, and advertising and containers in all sizes and prices. As in any collection field, at times certain store pieces are more in demand (for awhile, cash registers were very "in") and values shot up accordingly.

It is a moot point whether the items are worth the higher cost, and this is something each collector must decide. It is always best, however, to be guided more by quality than current market conditions. (In this field, as others, highest quality is investment-grade.) The second varies, while the first remains constant; the factor of quality endures. The essence of this collecting then is, first piece, second price.

Here are some observations on where and how store things can be obtained. Individual financial status decides the extent of collecting, sometimes the frequency, and certainly the category. Serious collectors usually have either a wide range of items, or a very representative collection in one or two narrow fields. Be that as it may, small store items tend to be lower-priced because there were many more of them, so they are more common and moderately priced.

Antiques shows are good for several reasons, one being that individual dealers have begun to carry small arrangements, general selections of store goods. Mostly — at least in the Midwest — these consist of tins, store-boxes, advertising, and a few large store fixtures. Prices tend to be competitive with other dealers, and that means (a bit of humor, but also fact) slightly more than the average collector likes to pay. But, "dickering" is not unheard of, and the word itself is an honored one. It means counting or bargaining on tens or two hands, counting fingers and finances.

Shows are good because they are regular events and well-announced in advance, giving the store collector plenty of notice. Shows tend to be somewhat of a problem, in that the word "show" should not be forgotten. It sometimes seems the emphasis is more on displaying high-priced collectibles rather than firmly keeping the collector in mind. This aside, the system works.

Antiques shops are the ongoing supplier of the trade, and store items are beginning to find their place in these enterprises. Unless the shop specializes in store items (see Ch. XI) these will be found in a small area to the side or rear of the shop. The pieces are usually grouped with advertising, tins, or anything that could be remotely associated with stores. Shop dealers are now aware of the great interest in store items, and many are beginning to include them.

There is in fact an inter-mixing of goods, all considered store items, which deserve mention. Some advertising was in magazines, these sheets now framed, that only came into the home. Some giveaways went directly to the purchaser (such as trade-cards or kitchen-related advertising utensils) and were not really store-involved. A few things, like baskets or air-tight storage containers, were used as much in the home as in the store. The collector must decide on this, whether the piece is store-only or, only store-related.

But, in the field today, if something was certainly a store piece, or likely was, or could have been, then it becomes "store" and is so-marked. "Store" in the item description seems to add a magical touch, making it more desirable and of course then more valuable. This includes, rightly or wrongly, anything with early advertising of any kind, in any way.

As collectors know, there is a great difference in antiques shops. Some personnel are as friendly and helpful as the old time country store proprietor, while others are as coldly polite as a foreclosing banker. It is very difficult to give an always-true analysis of antiques shops as sources for store items, but there is some worth in attempting one.

Large-city shops tend to have good items at high prices, while small-town shops seem to copy that trend. Rarely can a good store piece be purchased at much below the going rate. Sometimes the shops price store items far too high, as if trying to anticipate a coming trend or value increase. It is playing the stock market, country store stock, and the goods often go unsold. You will see them in the same shops a year later, often with the price reduced.

Small-town and rural antiques shops have less overhead and upkeep, and so goods may be more reasonably priced. Still, these dealers know their business, and prices tend to be "competitive", ie, like the other dealers.

One good possibility here is that the small antiques shop has obtained a collection or household inventory that wholesale dealers or "pickers" have not yet discovered, and the collector can find some excellent buys. An advantage is that the store goods are likely in fine condition, having been stored and protected for years. The disadvantage is, such finds either do not happen often, or are discovered first by other collectors.

Estate auctions can be productive, if the person was a store collector, or the family once operated one or more general stores. Often, large pieces with sentimental value (coffee grinders, cash registers) were kept in the family, and have now become available for the first time. Estate auctions tend to be well advertised, so other bidders may be after the same objects.

Competition here can drive the knock-down bid above fair market value, that being what a knowledgeable buyer and seller would agree upon. But, contact with other bidders in the same field is rewarding, since all have an interest in common. And everyone at least has the same chance to obtain a given item.

General antiques or collectibles auctions may have a few good store pieces, often not recognized as such by the average bidder. He or she may simply consider it something with a product or company name visible, and only of mild interest. All this is fine for the store collector, and good buys are possible on smaller objects. Large and dramatic store pieces often attract half-earnest bids even from non-collectors, who like the objects for home decoration. Store stuff is a well-understood part of the past, and even non-collectors are usually comfortable with the objects.

Some store-only auctions are held, and these seem to be of three kinds. First, and rare, is the store that ceased operations years ago, with contents now being sold. The goods tend to be in mint condition due to being protected. These stores and contents are up for auction because the owner or heirs have lost sentimental attachment to the store or have given up the idea of starting the store again. (It seems Americans are always either in business or out of business or between businesses.) Healthy bidding competition can be expected, if the sale has had at least average publicity.

Another store-only auction is the country enterprise currently closing down, having mostly modern merchandise. There is still the possibility of old and highly collectible items, especially store fixtures and furnishings that have been used all along. These include counters and display cases of all kinds. And, some very interesting things can be stored in basements and back rooms.

The big thing that is starting to happen is the specialized store auction. These may be multi-day sales with many hundred top grade store pieces, and collectors are attracted from other parts of the country. Well-advertised, such gatherings can both encourage sincere collector friendships, and engender strong interest in the better items. Top items are likely to be present — along with top prices. The collector need not be in this "advanced" league in order to attend sales and learn. Even if little is bid-in, such auctions can be considered a free educational class.

Shopping-mall shows have become increasingly popular, and there will usually be a scattering of store goods. These will be from low-cost tins to large and expensive store fixtures. These are sometimes brought in as much to attract attention to the particular dealer's booth or sales area as to be truly priced for a reasonably quick sale. It is interesting that some fixtures once designed to attract attention in the old stores have evolved to serve as sales aids for other, or related goods. The attraction remains.

The periodic shows in shopping malls have several spin-off ramifications. One is the mall store shoppers, who fall into three classes, and the collector will encounter them sooner or later. The first doesn't much care that the show is there, while the second objects to the crowded conditions caused by congestion. The third is intrigued by this new world of collectibles, and may even buy some store stuff.

However, here (as elsewhere) the collector may see the same dealer goods that have already been seen at other shops or shows. This is because dealers tend to make similar sales "circuits". The benefit however is that the collector can become friendly with certain dealers, and most are glad to keep alert for items in the collector's field of interest.

Another type of mall is the grouping of individual dealers in cities and towns, usually in some abandoned great old building, lodge-hall, school or factory, supermarket or auto dealership. Many kinds of antiques and collectibles are found under the roofs, and the chances that store items will be present are high. The good thing is that prices tend to be fairly reasonable. The bad thing is that these malls are rarely professionally managed, and dealing with them (whether as buyer or seller) can be both complicated and confusing. Yet, they provide one-stop shopping, or at least looking.

Flea markets are an established and growing part of buy-sell in America, and they are blossoming everywhere. It is very difficult to describe the average flea market, as the size and frequency and quality are very different. Some are great places to collect, while

Fine small under-counter collection of store-boxes and product containers, including tobacco, peanuts, tea, crackers and malted milk. As in all photos by Dan Poore, you will note that keys to advanced collecting include both choice of object — and top-grade condition.

Photo courtesy Dan Poore, Ft. Wayne, Indiana

Black-related store collectibles, a specialized field in itself. Left to right, coffee pails, plus tobacco, washing powders and boot-blacking box.

Photo courtesy Dan Poore, Ft. Wayne, Indiana

146

others are best avoided entirely. This is one area where the store collector must learn from personal experience and act accordingly.

Some fine materials can indeed be found, and many of the author's store pieces came from such sources. But flea markets can also be a waste of time and money unless one knows in advance approximately what will be found there.

If any two suggestions have validity, the first is, have cash, since some dealers are reluctant to take checks. Second, go early, before dealers and other collectors have purchased the bargains. There's little use in going late in the afternoon of the final day, whether one-day or week-end event. Then, the goods have been picked-over, and the dealers are tired and ready to go home.

Weather is a key. Clear, warm days bring out a feeling of well-being and generosity in both sellers and buyers. Bad weather induces an uptightness that puts everyone on edge, for heavy rain, high wind and lightning are not conducive to casual bargaining. On bad days, the dealers can be heard lamenting the low sales turn-over, but some are ready to discount merchandise to get cash for the homeward trip.

One of the most instructive of learning experiences is to become somewhat familiar with the buy-sell field of store items — and other antiques, for that matter. With a sharp eye and good memory, or ready notebook, jot down the piece/price at secondary auctions and and flea markets. Then see the exact, same items when they eventually appear in the "better" shops and shows. You will quickly understand that the shoe sign you saw for $40 was actually a $110 item. The mustard tin at $3 must have been rare, because there it sits with a $19 tag. In short, at times it may be best to buy as close as possible to the origin or source.

Yard sales are like small-scale flea markets, but with some differences. One can drive a great distance from one to another, expending the time and gas that, if directed toward a flea market, would have resulted in many more items being seen.

Yard and garage sales also vary in quality. Some are merely getting rid of varied accumulations, things past use by anyone, the last stop on the way to the dump. Others have a mix of collectibles, and some surprisingly good store finds have been made. People are becoming more aware of the value of collectibles, and often, before a yard sale, someone who "knows antiques" will help the seller by looking everything over and suggesting prices.

Too, collectors themselves have yard sales, and store goods can

147

then be found, but usually at just below antiques-shop prices. Or, duplicate items or unwanted objects can be offered at considerable savings over the show or shop prices. Yard-sale shopping, however, is fun and determined collectors often find treasures among the trash.

Perhaps the best way to acquire country store pieces is to go on an "expedition". There are certain places in the U.S. — such as the Reading, Pennsylvania, area — that have huge concentrations of antiques dealers and flea markets. Many hundred individual assemblages can be seen, housed in large buildings that sometimes include a farmers' market. Ads. for these appear in various collectors' publications, giving place, date, hours, and often, the number of dealers at each location.

In several days, one can see just about all the antiques and collectibles one cares to, endless thousands of items. These are truly mind-numbing affairs. Prices vary greatly, but tend to be reasonable. Many dealers can be seen obtaining stock for stores and shows. There are two tips of importance. First, if you plan to stay overnight in the area, call well ahead for motel reservations, because these quickly become filled. And, take plenty of money in a safe form (travelers' checks are ideal) because most people spend considerably more than they had planned. This is not only for food, gas and lodging, but for the collectibles. Store stuff, especially, can be seen everywhere.

At certain publicized times in the summer, larger outdoor flea markets are added to existing buildings and shops, with hundreds of more sellers. One can quite literally spend most of a day at just one, and still not see everything. Such trips are physically demanding, but — while more like work than fun — serious and dedicated collectors make such trips regularly.

Country store collectors sometimes neglect the most obvious sources or possibilities, by not letting friends and neighbors know they purchase store items. Often, collectors drive hundreds of miles to special events, not knowing there's a fine piece of two close to home. Social contacts of all kinds are often productive. This is the famous word-of-mouth advertising, and it costs nothing except a few words here and there.

This circle of information can be enlarged with an occasional classified ad. in the area newspaper, or in one of the national collectors' trade papers. And if one publication does not produce results, others can be tried. Ad. copy can be this simple: "Wanted — Old store items", followed by name and address. Or, if desired, the ad. can narrow the collecting field to whatever the person collects.

A selection of store and products ads., various sizes, with the Ox-Heart Chocolates & Cocoa" of particular interest because it is not widely known today.
Photo courtesy Dan Poore, Ft. Wayne, Indiana

Time of year has some impact on collecting sources. In northern states, yard sales are non-existent in the winter, but there are plenty of mall shows and special shows. However, in late winter dealers have had little chance (few auctions or flea markets) to replenish their stock. So, between, say, Christmas and Easter one is likely to see much the same material that was available just before the holidays.

Spring, summer and fall are all good, because everywhere, there is a vast exchange and intermixing of buyer and seller goods. Then, a vast number of store items are usually available for the collector.

Final tips for the store collector include these: Learn where the best buys are, and go there. Figure your time and mileage when computing bargain prices, plus gas and motels. If you come up short, consider the experience a mini-vacation, and keep at it. Collecting at heart should be fun, so remember to take advantage of parks and historic sites both to and from any collecting event. Store items involve good collecting and a valuable collection, but should also be a very pleasurable preoccupation.

Collecting, never forget condition. A small, mint tin may be a better value than a battered store fixture, however old or large or cheap. Stay also with what you know and are learning about, for the key to a good collection is knowledge and focus. Start a library of helpful books and magazines in your field, and during slow times read them as much as you can. Knowledge is sometimes as valuable as money, and often more so.

In short, the best tip possible to give a store collector is the ultimate collecting goal: Know what item is good, how good, and why.

Chapter XI

GENERAL STOCK

Here is a full shelf of additional store information. This material did not conveniently fit elsewhere in the book, but the sections are important enough to deserve appearance. This material will mainly be of interest to two collecting groups, beginners (Reproductions; Researching) and intermediate (Newsletter; Dealers). However, it will offer more than casual scanning for the average reader.

Newsletter

A Newsletter for country store collectors is being set up in the Midwest, but it should be of benefit nationwide. Also intended as a club for store-people, there are plans for regional chapters and an annual convention.

Collectors and those interested in store-related items are invited to contact the originator, Ms. Patricia McDaniel, P.O. Box 521, Connersville, Indiana 47321. For east of communication, please enclose an SASE when writing. In the author's opinion, this is a needed and worthwhile project.

Reproductions

Due to the popularity of "store stuff", there is a growing problem with reproductions in certain collecting fields. Of course, if one wishes to buy an item as a reproduction, and it is clearly marked as such, that is one thing. However, at some shows and flea markets, modern-made goods are intermixed with old pieces and are not marked. Then, it can be difficult for anyone not an expert to tell what is what.

In general, large, expensive and orate objects are not being reproduced. This includes cash registers, show-cases, cast-iron counter coffee grinders and the like. The reason seems to be that originals are still priced within reason, and reproductions cannot be made for these amounts.

What the collector must look out for are the smaller, much cheaper objects that are of simple construction and easy to mass-produce. These include many forms of signs and product-related advertisements, soft-driink items, ad. penknives, some of the store containers, and a number of photos. The photographs can be of store exteriors and/or interiors, and many are modern prints made from old black-and-white negatives.

Replica Stores

A growing number of people are establishing country stores, and many collectors have a room or two set aside, designed to look like part of an early store. It is possible to get some excellent ideas by visiting some of these stores, especially in regard to display methods and arrangements. Such authentic recreations can be seen in most of the many historic villages across the country. Sooner or later the store is added, for no frontier community was complete without one or several.

Researching

For a collection or display to accurately represent a certain era (say, ca. 1875) it is necessary either to be a very advanced collector, or to do research on just what was available for the period. And there are some excellent sources for that purpose.

National Park Service
U.S. Department of the Interior
NPS Photo by Richard Frear
74-1345-2
113-457

Appomattox Court House, an obscure village when Gen. Robert E. Lee surrendered the Army of Northern Virginia, was typical of the hundreds of hamlets throughout the South. Today the village closely resembles its 1865 appearance when the four-year old Civil War came to a close here at the McLean House.

Appomattox Court House
National Historical Park
Virginia

Interior of store built in 1850 by John Plunkett, and owned by Albert F. Meeks at the time of General Lee's surrender to end the Civil War. It is now known as the Plunkett-Meeks Store. Meeks used the ground floor as the general store, the basement for storage of goods, and lived with his family on the top floor. The interior of this store is from one at New Store that dates to 1865.

Photo courtesy Appomatox Court House National Historical Park, National Park Service, U.S. Department of the Interior

Store sign. Framed heavy paper stone lithograph, 28 x 64 inches. Extremely colorful, green, white, black, yellow and orange on red depicting "Chippewa Salt". (Chippewa Salt started as a turn-of-the-century product of the Ohio Salt Company, Wadsworth, Ohio, with company property located along Chippewa Creek. Morton Salt acquired the Corporation in 1948.) Sign pictures an Indian chief with feathered headdress. Mint condition, ca. 1915.

$175

Photo courtesy Dan Poore, Ft. Wayne, Indiana

Trade-card, front, "Gem Yeast Cakes", 4 x 5¾ in., colorful, mint condition.

$4

Private collection

Old newspaper advertisements are excellent, as are manufacturers' catalogs when they can be found. Ads. in early magazines are fine, since the publication's date establishes the exact period. Another good method is to locate a country store ledger of the time desired, and carefully study the pages. Individual family account books are useful in a similar fashion, but usually do not have the wealth of detail that the large store ledgers will contain.

The date of a company's founding is also a key. That is, if the business was founded in 1883, their products were not available in 1882. And if said company folded in 1894, their products in storage/liquidation were not likely sold more than a very few years after. Patent numbers, checked against records, will also give at least the patent date, which is not manufacture date.

Dealers

To aid the collector, here is a listing of a dozen top dealers who specialize in store-related collectibles. All agreed to be listed in the book, and most keep a good assortment of stock at all times.

Abby Brown's Sweet Shoppe
1415 E. State Blvd.
Ft. Wayne, Indiana 46805

Big Oaks General Store
1421 East 3rd St.
Hope, Arkansas 71801

Castle Rock Antiques
Rte. 2 - Box 35
Camp Douglas, WI 54618

Davis General Store
P.O. Box 26192
Birmingham, Alabama 35226

The Industrial Revolution
P.O. Box 25615
Chicago, Illinois 60625

Tom Mitchell
P.O. Box 3176
Vancouver, B.C.
Canada V6X-3X6

The Old Storefront Antiques
1839 Main / P.O. Box 261
E. Germantown, IA 47370

Olive Factory Antiques
6000 Auburn Blvd.
Citrus Heights, CA 95610

T. C. Packard
3775 Laurel
Studio City, CA 91604

Stonewall Antiques
221 S. Market St.
Loudonville, Ohio 44842

Tom's Hoard House
P.O. Box 6211
Santa Barbara, CA 93111

Yadkin Valley Country Store
Rte. 2 - Box 90-A
Norwood, NC 28128

A Personal Recollection

Mary Schmaltz's general store had the old gravity-empty glasstop gas pump out front in the early 1940's. After a scary ride (to a 5-year-old) on a plowhorse down from the high farm fields, I needed to go fishing. Hooks were two-for-a-cent, and I bought the largest from the box of loose hooks. I knew I was getting a lot for my money, forgetting that the hooks were nearly as big as what I hoped to catch in nearby White Eyes Creek.

I did better with the floppy straw hat, 15¢ then. To buy candy, I ran down the lane past the wild strawberries and evergreens, holding the pennies so hard they left an imprint in my palm. The nice thing about Mrs. Schmaltz was that she never seemed to mind when one took a long time making a decision at the candy case. Hats and hooks and much else — pleasant memories of store days.

The Old Country Store

Memory's lane leads back again,
To a simpler time and pace.
Where people came together,
The Store. A special place.

The keeper ruled a small domain,
Piled high and deep, 'tis true.
Whaddya need? Um. We got it!
At least, I think we do.

Working people came and went,
While loafers came and stayed.
All were welcome in The Store,
And sometimes, bills were paid.

It brought the mail in daily,
And always had the first 'phone.
If you needed to know it, or buy it,
The Store was a second home.

It never looked imposing,
The charm was all inside.
A country store of yesteryear,
Was yet a thing of pride.

All of that was long ago,
But, well, time travels on.
It fills a place in our days and hearts,
And now? And now it's gone.

Anon.